LUKE SKYWALKER CAN'T READ

And Other Geeky Truths

RYAN BRITT

A PLUME BOOK

PLUME
An imprint of Penguin Random House LLC
375 Hudson Street
New York, New York 10014
penguin.com

Illustrations © Wesley Allsbrook

LIBRARY OF CONGRESS CATALOGING-IN-PUBLICATION DATA
has been applied for.

ISBN 978-0-14-751757-9

Printed in the United States of America
10   9   8   7   6   5   4   3   2   1

Set in Esprit Std Book
Designed by Eve Kirch

For my dad

Those people who think they know everything
are a great annoyance to those of us who do.

—Isaac Asimov

CONTENTS

AUTHOR'S NOTE

This book isn't meant to be the final word on anything having to do with science fiction, fantasy, or any of those related fields. Others have written encyclopedically about all aspects of genre fiction and they've done it wonderfully. I think I try to do some of them justice here.

Instead, these essays simultaneously assume a little bit of familiarity with certain subjects (I think most people have seen *Star Wars*) but try to inform more on others. When it comes to *Doctor Who*, Isaac Asimov, Sherlock Holmes, or *Star Trek*, I tend to split the difference; sometimes there's a lot of background information in the essays, sometimes there's not. Occasionally, I've gone hog wild with the footnotes. This, I believe, simulates talking to me about these subjects, only less intensely.

Mostly, the aim of these essays is to add what I hope are new lenses to the conversations about various "geeky" topics. I've often found myself to be the only one saying a certain thing about a certain thing. And so, I decided to write it all down to not forget it. Other times, I've heard a common geeky opinion repeated over and over again, and I had to wonder why. As much as possible, I think I try to be fair, but these are only my opinions. Although I can't prove that I'm not a robot, I'm only human.

LUKE
SKYWALKER
CAN'T READ

Out of the Sideshows

When you're a kid in a 1994 junior high school locker room, and on the receiving end of towel-snaps and occasionally missing gym clothes, you also quickly pick up on a pervasive amount of slurs. Young boys call other boys terrible things: "queer," "wimp," and occasionally the uncreative and rote "looooser." But something that stung even worse than a towel-snap was often getting labeled a "nerd" or a "geek." Without getting too weepy or dramatic, I'll say being called these things sent a simple message: if there's a club where everyone agrees on being normal together, I wasn't in it.

If you use Google to find something other than a hip restaurant, looking up the word "geek" will reveal an etymological minefield. Katherine Dunn's excellent novel *Geek Love* is tragically not about having a crush on a girl who went to a Star Trek convention with me in 1992, but instead, about a family of circus freaks. Well, maybe replace "circus" with "sideshow" because the historical turn-of-the-nineteenth-century "geeks" were the performers who were often too ridiculous for the circus itself, mostly because their main job was to bite the heads off chickens, Ozzy Osbourne–style. If the boys in my junior high locker room were the circus, then I was in the sideshow: a segregated community in the kingdom of the unimportant.

But as the nerded and geeked boys and girls of the '80s and '90s have grown up and become pseudo-adults in this early section of the twenty-first century, we've noticed something odd: the Gap suddenly sells Star Trek T-shirts. Seemingly overnight, being a "geek" is cool and news article after blog post trumpets that now not only are geeks hip, but their hipness is here to stay, too. The geek(s) have inherited the Earth, which is why Star Trek, Star Wars, comic book heroes, and fantasy novels are more popular than ever. This, I believe, is broadly true, but there are various space-alien devils in the details, and it's in those details that I hope these essays live.

So, it's only fair I tell you now that I'm a bad geek, the same way Roxane Gay—smartly fearing the act of putting oneself on a pedestal—says she's a "bad feminist." I don't do or say or like all the things I'm supposed to, and I'm not beholden to any one fandom. I love Star Trek, but I hate the word "trekkie."* I'm obsessed with Sherlock Holmes, but am impatient that I've met almost no one who likes the Jeremy Brett adaptations as much as I do. I like *Doctor Who*, but I don't love *Firefly*. I like *The Avengers* and the rest of the Marvel Cinematic Universe explosion, but its dominance and the hype make me tired and occasionally cause uncontrollable eye rolls. Plus, my favorite

---

* "Trekker" is even worse.

Joss Whedon creation is the screenplay he wrote for *Alien: Resurrection*, which makes me super-unpopular with what I would characterize as more "conventional" geeks. I infamously love science fiction literature (contemporary and classic), but am also constantly complaining about how often the SF community ignores supposed mainstream fiction writers in our brave new genre-bending world.

And Star Wars. What to say about Star Wars? On the one gloved robotic hand, I'm like every Star Wars fan you ever met or could dream up: I collected the toys; I read the comics and novels. Hell, at fourteen years old, I even won a few tournaments of the 1996 Star Wars collectible card game. On the other, ungloved, fleshy hand, I'm also a hater, the Han Solo inside of Star Wars making fun of the absurdities contained in that far, far away galaxy. My closest friends and I wore homemade T-shirts to the midnight 2005 premiere of *Revenge of the Sith* with the words "George Lucas Is a Virgin" emblazoned on our chests. "Real" Star Wars fans weren't sure what we meant. Did we hate Star Wars? (No.) Did we think George Lucas was so bad at writing dialogue that it seemed like he'd never had sex? (Yes.) Were we making fun of everyone by wearing these shirts? (Yes and no.) Why would someone camp out for a movie only to mock other people who were also camping out for said movie? (Unclear.)* Being the kind of geek I am is weird and confusing, but I'll attempt to prep you for what you're in for by telling you that on that very same night I also made out with Jar Jar Binks.

---

* And it will become even more unclear in the essay "Imagine There's No Frodo."

When the whole prequel thing started in 1999, the release of *Star Wars Episode I: The Phantom Menace* was famously preceded by an avalanche of toylike merchandise intended to get you to care about this new slew of characters, most of which you'd never heard of, including but not limited to a pilot named Ric Olie,* a Frog-man named Boss Nass, Liam Neeson with "hippie poncho action," and, of course, the lovable clown of this particular science fiction circus: Jar Jar Binks. Someone apparently thought Jar Jar's long, gross tongue was funny, because there are no less than three bits in the movie featuring his tongue doing things that are *hilarious*. But that's not the worst of it, because there was also a Jar Jar candy product. It was a plastic holder shaped like Jar Jar's face, and when you pressed a button, his jaws opened and his tongue shot out. His tongue was a candy that you were supposed to eat. This is a real thing. I have pictures. You were supposed to lick Jar Jar's tongue to eat this special Star Wars candy.

One of my closest friends and I—both still in high school at the time—thought this was staggeringly hysterical precisely because it was obviously in such poor taste. Star Wars was jumping the space shark way before the movie even came out. There and then, we bought enough of a supply of the Jar Jar tongue candies so that we could eat them in the theatre right before Episode III began. So, six years later, wearing our George

---

* Seriously, pre–*Phantom Menace* hype leaned heavily on this "character," a guy who is really only in the movie for like three seconds where he just says, "There's the blockade!" He was played by an actor named Ralph Brown who has actually had a respectable career since, including guest spots on *Elementary* and *Life on Mars*. He was also in *Alien 3*. Go figure.

Lucas T-shirts, I toasted my friend Justin and we each licked the tongue of our respective Jar Jars. We sucked on Jar Jar's tongue and got ready to see what (we thought) was going to be the last Star Wars movie ever. And if any of that makes sense to you, then you'll understand the kind of geek I am. I'm in the club, but I'm doing the Groucho Marx thing of being suspicious of any Jedi order that would have me as a member. There are no real geeks, and there are no "fake" geeks either.

In a great comedy called *Adam's Rib*, Katharine Hepburn says this better than I can, and if you feel so inclined, anytime I quote anyone in this book—from science fiction author to fantasy character to unlikely scholar—I entreat you to imagine it in Katharine Hepburn's voice. In the scene that I like most of all, Hepburn is trying to get her secretary to agree with her on a particular point about this woman they're defending who shot (but didn't kill!) her husband. Hepburn is angry that her lackey isn't chiming in with any opinion at all. The lackey says, "I don't make the rules," to which Hepburn barks back, "Sure you do, we *all* do."

We all make the rules. And that includes how we define words like "sci-fi," "fantasy," and "geek." In his essay "Science Fiction," Kurt Vonnegut said that the crowd of science fiction writers only exist because science fiction writers want it that way: "They are joiners. They are a lodge. If they didn't enjoy having a gang of their own so much, there would be no such category as science fiction. They love to stay up all night, arguing the question 'What is science fiction?'"

Samuel R. Delany came up with a handy definition of

science fiction in his essay "About 5,750 Words,"* in which he claims that "naturalistic fictions are [just] parallel world stories in which the divergence from the real is too slight for historical verification." Meaning, *Wuthering Heights* takes place in an alternate universe where a guy named Heathcliff is a massive asshole and *Moby-Dick* takes place in an alternate universe in which whale attacks were a common enough thing to get upset about. In this way, every kind of fiction is science fucking fiction, which means that everybody who likes reading anything that's not nonfiction is a massive geek.

Obviously, like a lot of geeks, my hyperbole is worse than my bite. Because even Delany had more to say about the definition of science fiction, speculative fiction, or fantasy than just that. And like Vonnegut's bygone cronies, or a million other people, I do love to stay up late (and often get up early) to argue the question of what science fiction is, often in the form of an essay like this one. But I'm not one of those joiners Vonnegut talks about and I think that it's a truism that even those geeks who appear to be joiners aren't really joiners either. Vonnegut is half-right, because science fiction, and by extension all "geek" communities, is real not just because there are people who claim it, but because there are plenty of people who still mock it. For every one person who says that "being a nerd is cool," there are plenty who casually and dismissively say, "I don't really like science fiction."†

---

* From *The Jewel-Hinged Jaw.*

† In "A Fictional Architecture" (also from *The Jewel-Hinged Jaw*), Delany insinuates this statement is code-speak for people who don't know any better. I'd like to think this book you're holding is for those people, too.

The late great Ray Bradbury uttered the definitive geek battle cry for dealing with the naysayers who don't "get" geeky interests when he said, "I never listened to anyone who criticized my taste in space travel, sideshows, or gorillas. When this occurs, I pack up my dinosaurs and leave the room."

Look! It's those pesky sideshows again, the place where the original geeks came from, at least one origin of why being interested in science fiction, fantasy, dinosaurs, and all the stuff that comes with it makes people feel ostracized and left out. I guess it was rougher for Bradbury growing up literally almost one hundred years ago, but I think he got lucky. Not only did he go on to create some of the best books in any genre ever; he also was childhood friends with Ray Harryhausen, a man who literally brought stop-motion monsters to life. Contemporarily, this would be like J. K. Rowling going to high school and being best friends with J. J. Abrams. But not all of us are so lucky as children, and maybe sometimes, even as adults. Maybe there's not a comic con near us, or maybe those gatherings aren't quite what we want. Maybe even today, with the widespread acceptance of *Game of Thrones*, or literally, every Marvel superhero ever created, there's still a geek-shunning. And if you think I'm wrong, then why are we still using the word "geek"? It's still easy to take potshots at "geeky" interests, though it's getting harder, which is why I'm even able to write this book in the first place.

Part of it, I think, isn't just waiting for the world to change, but holding our ground. Because unlike Bradbury, I don't pack up and leave the room. I *stay in the room*. And I talk. Which I think explains the rest of "geek" culture becoming more mainstream than it was in the previous century, and a lot of factors conspired to make it happen. J. K. Rowling didn't pack up and go anywhere. And neither did Russell T. Davies when he approached the BBC about bringing back *Doctor Who*. And neither did George Lucas in 1977. They stayed in the room. They talked about their Muggles and Time Lords and Jedi Knights. They stood up for their geekery and flew their freak flags in ways that transformed us all. They didn't put their ideas in a box, or a genre. They decided these things were destined to come out of the sideshows and they were right.

What I mean about staying in the room isn't just about standing up to non-geeks. Oftentimes, the people I'm talking to about the things I love aren't ignorant or haters, but other geeks, too. We need to figure out why we like the stuff we like! Just because something is "geeky" doesn't make it good and it's our job as geeks (of any variety) to question all this stuff, to think about it, and to hold it up to a standard beyond simple genre definitions. On message boards, I'll sometimes see people say things like "It's an epic fantasy, it's supposed to have bad dialogue." Or "It's a space opera, it's not supposed to make sense." And so on. We can never afford to be clichés in these circles, because the world is all too willing to take those clichés and turn them into unfunny monsters.

Geeks, nerds, fangirls, fanboys, and just plain old *fans*, all have the same duty. Stay in the room. Recognize we all make the rules. I, of course, think I'm right. But I'm not right forever, and someone, I'm sure, will prove me wrong about one of my many "truths" in this book. That's the idea. That's what's *supposed* to happen. This is the beginning of a conversation and I hope you have fun. Maybe you're a bad geek and maybe I am one, too. Maybe you're not a geek at all. Maybe you're my sister, who is, somehow, not a geek. Maybe you're a superintelligent robot from the future, trying to determine which human texts from 2015 you should upload into your hivemind starship. Whatever the case, welcome. It's 2015. And we're all geeks. But, maybe just maybe, we'll not need that word someday. Maybe we'll give it up, because now that we're out of the sideshows, done with being picked on, comfortable with our dinosaurs and gorillas, we'll give up the label. Maybe someday it will be different. Before Doc Brown took the DeLorean into the future of 2015 at the end of *Back to the Future*, he famously said, "Roads? Where we're going we don't need *roads*." A road is just a constraint, a direction, a category. Maybe the same will be true for this. Maybe someday we'll invent new words for "science fiction," "fantasy," and "geek."

And I suspect that day is right now, because you might know "right now" by its other name. The future.

The Birds, the Bees, and *Barbarella*

Walking in on your parents having sex is one thing, but walking in on a couple of dinosaurs is something else. It's not necessarily worse, just a little unexpected, particularly if you are not a dinosaur. When we're kids, figuring out the whole deal with sex is not a mystery we're all trying to solve; it's just something that never occurs to us. It's like asking, "How come Superman gets away with just putting on the glasses?" You don't ask questions apropos of nothing until later, when you're confronted with them, almost by accident. And my accidental "birds and bees" talk was precipitated by seeing some dinos get it on.

Shocking no one, this sex act wasn't in real time, nor was it shaky-cam footage of real dinosaurs. I'm sad to say I don't have any good intel on secretly living prehistoric creatures, though I do know people with Bigfoot fetishes. This dino-sex-act came from a magazine, an old issue of the science/science fiction magazine *Omni*, dated October 1988, which would have made me seven years old. Along with *Playboy* and *Penthouse*, my father also subscribed to *Omni*, which I loved because it always had my favorite stuff in it: spaceships, aliens, and dinosaurs. But in this issue, the dinosaurs were doing something I'd never seen dinosaurs do before: they were getting on top of each other in what looked like a sort of weird, horizontal piggyback ride. All my favorites, too: apatosauruses (brontosauruses), tyrannosauruses, triceratops. Were they smiling? This was before we all knew about raptors, so all dinosaurs to a kid in the '80s were really huge. Wouldn't that hurt to have one on top of you? Even if you were another dinosaur?

The illustrations were done by an artist named Ron Embleton and the article itself was written by Sandy Fritz and was titled "Tyrannosaurus Sex: A Love Tail." My child brain processed the basics of the illustrations—one dinosaur on top of another dinosaur—and I could read the words, but none of it was making any sense. It was like learning Santa Claus isn't a real person or *Godzilla* isn't actually a documentary. I needed it explained to me. And my father was happy to oblige.

"Dinosaurs were just like people," he said. "When they really loved another dinosaur, they would diddle them, and make more dinosaurs." My dad wasn't embarrassed about talking about sex one bit, and looking back, it seems like he was dying for an excuse to faux-innocently broach the topic and use the word "diddle."

"So, dinosaurs had to love each other to make other dinosaurs?" I said.

"Well . . ." my dad said.

"So did they all die because they stopped loving each

other?" My dad considered this for a second, gently stroking his period-appropriate Tom Selleck mustache.

"Maybe the love part wasn't the important thing," he said, "but what they *did* because of it."

In my childhood and adolescence, science-y stuff and science fiction in particular always seemed to be a weird portal into knowledge about sexuality and adulthood, my wardrobe leading into a naked and deranged Narnia. My parents were strange sociopolitical hybrids from another dimension, totally godless Republicans (we *never* went to church) who maintained strict bedtimes and rigorous chore schedules, but let my sister and me absorb all sorts of racy media, just as long as it wasn't too violent. My father didn't exactly leave the *Playboy*s and *Penthouse*s lying around all the time, but it was known to happen. He was a photographer, so I think he and my mother tried to cultivate a half-assed "The Human Body Is Beautiful" philosophy, which they implemented as well as their We-Used-To-Be-Hippies-But-Now-We-Love-Reagan sensibilities allowed. This is to say that my mom was still a mom and my dad was still a dad, meaning when my dad would try to get away with some bullshit, my mom would call him on it. Which is where *Barbarella* comes in.

Barbarella. 1968. Jane Fonda, who plays the titular character, is in space boots, and little else, brandishing a ray-gun and looking like a sci-fi soft-core porn supernova. If you're unfamiliar, I'm not sure you necessarily *need* to see it, but it is, kind of, a science fiction classic. This isn't to say that it's good—like at all—it's just that when it comes to "important" science fiction and fantasy, the larger pop canon of science fiction and fantasy tends to include all sorts of great stuff alongside some total shit that is really memorable, and also, well, *good* in a different way. *Lost in Space*, for example, is objectively terrible, and yet, it had that great robot and a family who lived on a flying saucer, so it becomes "important." *Lost in Space* next to an episode of the classic *Star Trek* is exactly like the fact that box wine is sold in the same store as some delicious Barolo. I just know when I'm slumming it. And sometimes, you might just want to grab the box wine because it's easier.

This, I think, more than anything, is what has historically turned off a lot of people from sci-fi and fantasy: the inability to see the value in the crappier examples while simultaneously being unable to distinguish it from the supposed "good stuff." As I mentioned, those *Playboy*s were sometimes lying around my house growing up, but because of my dad's photographer status so was a black-and-white instructional manual called *Nude Photography: The French Way*. When I hit puberty, I actually preferred the ladies in *Nude Photography: The French Way* to those in an issue of *Playboy*. Can this distinction really be the difference between "good" sci-fi/fantasy and "trash"? Kind of. And what's worse is that it's made even more confusing when you consider that truly trailblazing genre authors like Margaret Atwood and Ursula K. Le Guin were (and still are!) published in *Playboy*. The mix of lowbrow "trash" with high-concept "brilliance" is the undeniable heritage of science fiction and fantasy, and it's totally connected with a young person's notions of growing up. Which—duh—is connected to sex.

The idea that those of us who end up loving science fiction and/or fantasy are obsessed with the low-hanging fruit when we're young is tricky, because all kids are obsessed with low-hanging fruit. They're kids! And if you're still into that stuff—robots, aliens, and dinos—as an adult it can come across as a bit like you haven't really grown up. As a grown-up, I'm lucky to have a lot of friends who are totally into the whole cosplay scene: they dress up as characters from their favorite fiction. One couple I know tends to do couples costumes, and my favorite one was when they dressed as Luke Skywalker and Han Solo, partly because this couple is a couple of girls. Other times, they'll dress up as something more highbrow: maybe characters from the book versions of *Dune*. The kind of geek you are depends on the day, and your mood. Box wine or Barolo.

So where the hell does *Barbarella* fit in? At a glance, *Barbarella* is an on-purpose crappy movie with the pornographic trappings of embarrassingly old-school testosterone-fueled science fiction. And yet, somehow, for me anyway, it's accidentally a progressive work of sci-fi genius. *Barbarella*—the film—is like an idiot savant, maybe not aware it's good (and often bad in many places) and maybe not even actually good, but infinitely redeemable. A Rosetta stone for explaining how we think about pop fiction. Barbarella—the person—is essentially a female James Bond, somebody who is fucking people to get what she wants and definitely not with the intention of making little Barbarellas. From her first moments in a zero-gravity striptease, nine-year-old me started to connect the dots between sex as a sometimes reproductive act and sex as recreation. The dinosaurs-doing-it-for-fun comment my dad had made a few years earlier started to make a little more sense. Just because you get your birds-and-bees (and brontosauruses) talk doesn't mean you instantly understand sex, the universe, and everything, overnight. In 1990, I was a tiny bit worldlier than when I'd stumbled on "Tyrannosaurus Sex," but still at not quite ten years old, I still hadn't figured out my body, or science fiction. To be fair, at thirty-three, there's a very real chance that I still haven't done either.

Barbarella had a profound effect on me. There's something fairly guiltless about enjoying this movie, because it's so obviously about sex. And yet, in being exposed to it so young, I was getting the good stuff about the movie without any of the horny and misogynistic baggage. Sure, I was starting to feel certain stirrings by watching this movie, but little kids have so much weird sexual energy, that was inevitable. The profound thing about *Barbarella* was that I was tricked into renting it by my father.

When we went to the video store with one parent or the other, either my sister or I was allowed to pick out "our own" movie, while whichever parent was with us got something else. For a solid five years, this probably meant I lurked in the sci-fi/fantasy/horror section of a non-franchised hole-in-the-wall called the Movie SuperStore. Mostly I stuck with certified classic monster movies—*Frankenstein, Creature from the Black Lagoon, The Wolf-Man*—which my parents supported because these films were usually bloodless. You could call this policy "boobs not blood," but prior to *Barbarella*, it was mostly just blood. The day this happened, though—sometime in December 1990, I think—I had my little paws on something that was probably

Godzilla vs. the Cosmic Monster or some similar fare, which I had certainly already seen. (Side note: isn't it funny how little kids cling desperately to the familiar? Next to the very elderly, they've got to be the most set in their ways of any age group.) But my dad was like, no *Godzilla*, what about *Barbarella*?

"You'll like this!" he said. "It's got all your favorite stuff in it."

"Dinosaurs?" I said.

"No, but spaceships and ray-guns and, look, this guy can fly!" I had to admit, Barbarella's ray-gun did look awesome, and everything else about the movie seemed appealing. When we got home my mother rolled her eyes really hard when she saw what I had selected as "my movie."

"Ryan picked this out, huh?" she snorted. "All on his own?"

"What?!" my dad said. "He's gonna love it."

"I bet he's not the only one," my mom said.

In that moment, *Barbarella* became my first guilty pleasure. I did like it a lot, though I never really let on to my mom that I did. And in my heart, I knew I really didn't understand it, but that it was *changing* me. When Jane Fonda has an orgasm so strong that she breaks the "Excessive Machine," I had no idea what was going on. Did I understand the lesbian tendencies between her and the Black Queen of Sogo? Nope. Was the joke of the name Dildano lost on me? Yep. And was I, like many of you, thoroughly confused about the search for someone named Duran Duran?* Yes, the band got its name from this

---

* Technically, the name of the character in the film is "Dr. Durand Durand," played by Milo O'Shea. The band ditched the final *d*'s.

movie; the movie was not searching for the band, even though, philosophically, it kind of was.

Somehow, because Barbarella was a girl, and seemed to sort of be *in charge of the movie*, and won through less-than-conventional means, I think it made me start to think differently about what to expect from these kinds of stories. And maybe other stuff, too. Ironically, because I was sort of still figuring out some of the sex-stuff in the movie, I could draw my own conclusions from it that my father, the supposed *Barbarella* fan, was totally incapable of. I don't think this was the result he had hoped for. I think his goal was to turn me into a sort of man's man, kind of like him. This didn't really work, because what I took away from the movie ended up having little to do with what my father loved about it. He created a monster, totally by accident.

In watching *Barbarella* as an adult, and science fiction critic, I've realized that my thinking about sci-fi/fantasy started right here. For little kid me, this wasn't a movie that I'd wanted. It didn't reinforce anything that I really had enjoyed about these types of stories at that time—male main character, outer space morals, people who were clothed—which is exactly why it changed me. By throwing sex in the viewer's face and having a woman seemingly not be the victim of it, the movie tried to convey (a little naive) '60s progressivism, which was actually lost on someone like my father, who was of that generation. In 1990, as a sort of armchair Larry Flynt conservative, my father just saw the movie as an excuse to watch soft-core porn at dinnertime. For my father, *Barbarella* was wish fulfillment, getting away with something, reinforcing his own interpretation of what the movie was about. But for me, it was a sea change, something that was in the category of stuff I liked, but totally different. Because it was so imperfect and so odd and full of stuff I didn't understand, it was more of a challenge, and it required me to pay better attention, and think about life in ways I never had before. A *woman* could run the show, a *blind man* could fly, and maybe the astronaut you're trying to rescue will turn out to be an asshole. I know feminists are divided on this movie, but count me among the feminists who think the good outweighs the bad for this particularly confusing mess of pop culture. And that's because *Barbarella* is exactly like a short story by Margaret Atwood appearing in an issue of *Playboy*, a mixed message that requires the individual to parse out the good from the bad, the low-hanging fruit from the potential for intellectual and emotional growth.

Soon after this epic viewing, my father (who passed away in 2012) offered me his definition of what science fiction supposedly "really was." He'd repeat this notion well into my adulthood.

"You've got to have three things," he said, "spaceships, robots, and babes. Otherwise, it's not science fiction *I* want to watch." It goes without saying that my dad liked Robert Palmer music videos.

Luckily, I didn't really listen. I had those blameless, noneroticized dinosaurs as my first introduction to sex way before he told me this particular brand of dad-malarkey. And by the time he did say it, I'd already started to make up my mind differently about *Barbarella* anyway. Liking that movie taught me what I've found profound about science fiction and fantasy:

just because someone else defines "it" for you, doesn't mean you can't redefine it for yourself.

My father had a limited, totally backward, and incorrect view of science fiction, but he still managed to introduce me to great stuff, even if by accident. Loving the good with the bad is part of what it means to love sci-fi and fantasy, and just like realizing dinosaurs could love to diddle, I was starting to figure out there was a whole lot more to robots, sex, and life itself than what my dad or even Jane Fonda and her ray-gun could teach me.

I Know It's Only Science Fiction,
but I Like It

Science fiction became rock and roll for me when I was seventeen, in the summer of 1999. Just before heading into my senior year of high school, I was pulling shifts at a big-box bookstore in Phoenix, Arizona, where I'd close the place four nights a week with my manager and personal hero at the time, Captain Space Pirate.

Outrageously handsome, thirtyish, with a dark mop of hair and a beard, and always dressed all in black, Captain Space Pirate was basketball-player tall, but hunched over in the way he'd probably done since burying his nose in books in grade school. This gave his handsomeness an Ichabod Crane resemblance. I didn't know about Space Pirate Captain *Harlock*—the anime character—at the time, but that visage plus a beard isn't far off. He drove a motorcycle to work and wore a black leather jacket, which, when taken off, revealed his black button-up and black skinny tie. He was a superhero mash-up of the Hamburg leather-wearing Beatles you see in those really old photos and the clean-cut Beatles on *Ed Sullivan*. And because he was the only person back then who knew more about Star Trek and Star Wars than I did, Captain Space Pirate was about as rock and roll as it got.

This might not be exactly proof that he was cool, but my mom totally had a crush on him. Though I usually drove myself to work in my 1987 Gold Dodge Ram 50 pickup truck—complete with an X-Wing fighter window decal, unironically affixed above a sticker for the band Oasis—one day I was forced to carpool with my mom so she could take my truck on some other errand after dropping me off. On that day, she went out of her way to go into the bookstore and give my boss, Captain Space Pirate, a hug. "It's the smile," she'd say when talking about him later. "He smiles like Indiana Jones."

Captain Space Pirate told me he'd long ago dated one of the actresses from *Buffy the Vampire Slayer* before she was famous, but wouldn't tell me which one. He told me he'd seen eleven different cuts of *Blade Runner* the year it was released. He told me that the novel version of *Star Wars: From the Adventures of Luke Skywalker*, by George Lucas, was really written by a guy named Alan Dean Foster, even though Lucas's screenplay came first. Captain Space Pirate's girlfriend was only a little bit older than I was and I thought their age gap was terribly odd, but I internalized it all as part of what made my manager great. At that point, his girlfriend knew more about vampires than anyone I'd known.

He also gave me a break. Technically, Captain Space Pirate shouldn't have hired me at this bookstore at all, because it was against the larger company policy to take on anyone under eighteen. But he'd given me a job because I'd consistently attended the geeky gaming nights and Star Wars book club stuff since the age of fourteen. When I got the job, I couldn't believe my luck: I was getting paid to read books and talk about Star Wars all day long. I was beginning my rock-and-roll fantasy of living in the protected world of geeky stuff I loved, surrounded only by people who "got it." And, prepare to be shocked: plenty of my co-workers claimed that they did in fact "get it."

The year 1999 was a very good one for hot-blooded geeks getting their ire up about all the things they hated to love and all the things they loved to hate. If you've seen *High Fidelity*, then you're familiar with a certain amount of overly informed pseudo-intellectual banter that pervades a place where people are way more into the things than the people they're selling them to. Jack Black's character, Barry, epitomizes this in *High Fidelity*: someone who is such a snob that he won't sell a certain record to a patron because the patron doesn't like it the "right" way. At my bookstore, we had four sci-fi Barrys on any given shift, all quick to cut me down to size about my severely underdeveloped opinions on everything from *Star Trek* to *Babylon 5* to the death of Superman to whether or not the *Dune* series is inherently ruined by virtue of the fact that it's read at all. Back then (and occasionally, shamefully, now) I was sometimes that guy, too, the snob accidentally lecturing someone about the "real" Buck Rogers or why a certain interpretation of Batman or Sherlock Holmes "sucks."

Captain Space Pirate, however, was too soft, too sweet, to correct me the way some of the other angry clones would. He wasn't bitter or jaded, but instead steady and tolerant of my nerd-rage outbursts. If I wanted to pretend to know everything about the history of werewolf films, Captain Space Pirate would simply allow me to embarrass myself on my own, letting me stick my own monster-clawed foot into my ignorant young mouth.

Notably, for complicated hormonal, contrarian reasons, I'd decided to come out as an iconoclast and pretend like I totally hated the at-the-time-brand-new movie *The Matrix*, even though, objectively speaking, it was awesome. In case you forgot: *The Matrix* is a 1999 movie in which Keanu Reeves lives an ordinary, boring life, only to learn his real life is fake and everyone in the world is actually strapped into a big old computer program being controlled by aliens. And the jam is, once Keanu is in the good part of "the Matrix" he can do all sorts of crazy kung fu stuff and essentially turn into a rapid-punch video game character while listening to songs from Rob Zombie, Marilyn Manson, or—wait for it—Rage Against the Machine. And very lazily, I hated it. I told myself that this whole Matrix thing was messy and filled with bad angsty music, which made it all way too close to home. *The Matrix* was science fiction, but because I personally couldn't actually escape into it, I decided it didn't do science fiction "the right way" and overreacted by telling all my fellow Barrys that it was "crap." The easiest way to do this was to make claims leaning on a fake sense of superiority and imagined sci-fi education I affected that I already possessed. I'd say things like "it's not original" and then sort of just imply that everyone knew there must be some sort of crusty old sci-fi text from which *The*

Matrix ripped off all its good ideas. To be clear: I wasn't *actually* sure this was true, but chose to act like I was right anyway. It's backward science: here's my hypothesis, don't bother checking my research, and now, let me get mad that you don't agree! I guess I figured everyone else was totally full of shit, too, and since no one was really keeping track of this stuff, it probably didn't matter if I was right or wrong about *The Matrix*. The thing to do was to have an opinion, and if you were a true geek, the default opinion was probably always going to be negative. This, more than anything, explains the painful popularity of the character of Comic Book Guy on *The Simpsons*, who is always dismissively declaring everything the WORST THING EVER!

I imagine I made life very difficult for Captain Space Pirate with all of my bullshit back then. Probably one of the reasons Luke Skywalker is such a compelling character is because Mark Hamill plays him so specifically without irony in the first *Star Wars* film. Luke alternates between eager to please one minute and whiny and questioning the next. It might seem like an inconsistency in his character, but it's beautifully accurate to what it's like to be young and a "rebel without a cause." Even before the Imperial Stormtroopers murder Luke's family,* he's a frustrated, angry person. Once his aunt and uncle are reduced

---

* I don't subscribe to the "popular" Internet theory that Boba Fett killed Luke's aunt and uncle. And for all the reading-into I do in this book, I think in this case, the simplest explanation is the correct one. Obi-Wan says, "Only Imperial Stormtroopers are so precise." That's it for me. I also dislike the Boba Fett theory because it doesn't say anything *else* about Star Wars or our culture or the impact of anything on anything. It's just bizarre faux-continuity porn. Which I'm usually all for. Just not with Boba Fett.

to smoking skeletons, he's got an excuse, but most of us don't have that. We're just pissed-off adolescents. Maybe you were, but I was, definitely. There's a great Louis C.K. joke about how guys on first dates try on "all kinds of other guys," while attempting to figure themselves out, and I think that's what Luke Skywalker is doing in his first outing, and I think that's what a lot of us do as teenagers. Regurgitating half-baked opinions from things we've read, while trying to piece together what kind of person we might be. Luke had Obi-Wan Kenobi to steer him in the right direction, and I had Captain Space Pirate.

As far as actual work-in-the-bookstore stuff went, Captain Space Pirate didn't run a tight ship at all, and I often got the impression that he was under a lot of pressure from his corporate superiors to get his merry band of disaffected nerds to actually shelve the books properly. You'd think the Star Wars books would be organized. And because I was generously assigned to organize the science fiction and fantasy book section, you'd think that I would have made sure everything there was tops. Instead, it was a *mess*. An unruly joke factory, a bookseller's nightmare combined with the kind of disorganization necessitating hypnosis for librarians to repress.

◆

I'll never know if Captain Space Pirate sabotaged his motorcycle that one night, or whether it genuinely wouldn't start, but the net result was that I had to give him a ride home, and we had to load his motorcycle into the back of my pickup truck. Captain Space Pirate lived forty-five minutes away in a housing community where he was that guy on the urban- planning board who would wonder aloud why they wouldn't let him paint his house all black. We talked about this a little on the drive, but also about work. This is when he asked me why my section wasn't really as organized as it could be.

"So what's the deal with the Star Wars books?" he said, and my memory has added that he's holding a cigarette, even though he really didn't smoke.

"What do you mean?" I said, merging onto the U.S. 60 while turning down "One Headlight," by the Wallflowers, on the radio.

"It's a fucking mess, man."

"Is it?"

"Yeah," he said. "And you know, I don't really care, but I thought you'd at least try a little harder when it came to the things you're actually interested in. I mean, of all the people that work there, you're the most qualified to make that section look better."

"But nobody cares, man," I said, feeling guilty, and doing what all teenagers do when they're guilty: fight back.

"Well, I care."

When Captain Space Pirate threw a Luke Skywalker quote back in my face, I knew something needed to change. I realized something right then that would inform how I viewed not just my own adult life, but science fiction and fantasy specifically. The angry nerds we worked with at the bookstore might not care if the Star Wars books were organized properly, and the average customer might not give a damn either, but Captain Space Pirate *noticed* and I should, too. Just because something is silly, or is involved with dubious standards of legitimacy— like science fiction and fantasy—doesn't mean you don't take it seriously. Which is exactly like real rock and roll.

Living a rock-and-roll lifestyle sometimes means sex, drugs, and being irresponsible, but people have to take their music seriously to actually exist, to matter. You know, to be rock stars. Being angry or contrarian about sci-fi and fantasy wasn't enough. My friend and mentor was holding me to a higher standard, one that meant I wouldn't devolve into being someone who just started arguments by declaring something was or was not "the worst thing *ever.*" Being rock and roll means a little more than just breaking guitars on a stage, since you've got to know how to play that guitar in the first place. And thanks to Captain Space Pirate, I realized a lot of our buddies were just breaking guitars without knowing what to do with them. Science fiction and fantasy was our rock and roll and it was up to us to do it right.

By the time I turned eighteen, that particular corporate bookstore had an incompressible magazine section, a ridiculously mis-shelved philosophy section, and a self-help section that would actually cause people to have new emotional breakdowns. But the science fiction/fantasy section was now *meticulous.* In an era before *Wikipedia* could guide me, I'd created subgenres other branches of our chain bookstore wouldn't have dreamed of, and within a specific author section, the book titles were no longer shelved alphabetically. No, no, no. Now, those titles were shelved in publication order, meaning back then, we had *The Chronicles of Narnia* in what many today would consider the "right" order.

When it came to the Star Wars books, though, doing it by author or publication order made zero sense, and here, Captain Space Pirate was super-impressed with what I'd come up with. Back then, when the Internet was more like a bad special effect than something pervading our real life, I'd put the Star Wars books in an order I'm fairly confident existed only in a handful of other places at the time. Just as John Cusack's Rob organizes his records "autobiographically" in *High Fidelity*, I put the Star Wars books in a specific reading order; each section told the specific biography of a particular character. There was a small Han Solo section; a section for books that were more Princess Leia–centric; a section for some of the anthologies out at the time that focused on the minor, briefly seen characters; a Chewbacca section; plus larger stretches of shelves for Luke, and his dad, Darth Vader.

Meanwhile, was I right about *The Matrix*? Well, as a real adult, I've come up with a fairly comprehensive Matrix rip-off list, including a good chunk on William Gibson's cyberpunk stuff and the famous 1967 Harlan Ellison story "I Have No Mouth and I Must Scream." In that particular short story, people are tortured by a gleefully malevolent computer program that hates them. The story ends with a dude literally being turned into a blobby thing that doesn't have a mouth, like Keanu losing his mouth at the start of *The Matrix*.

I've never lost my big mouth, but I did figure out having one wasn't the thing that made science fiction like rock and roll. Instead, you had to really *be cool* to be cool. Like Captain Space

Pirate, I figured out the best way to look at this stuff is to wear your leather jacket over your button-down and tie, and to talk about science fiction like it is the only thing that matters, but know your stuff, too. Even if you loved Star Wars, you probably wouldn't have noticed my bizarrely nuanced shelving system, which evokes that age-old question: if you can speak perfect Ewokese but there's not an Ewok around to hear it, does it still count as perfect? I think Captain Space Pirate knew the answer, and after that summer, so did I.

Luke Skywalker Can't Read

Growing up, I thought I was just like Luke Skywalker. While Luke lived on a desert planet called Tatooine and I lived in a desert suburb called Mesa, Arizona, we were both weirdo loners with outsider interests, and we both longed for adventures that were seemingly prohibited by our sweaty, outdoor, sunburn-causing chores. I bet about a billion little girls and boys felt (and feel) the same way as I did. When Luke Skywalker stares off into the setting suns while the strings of John Williams swell and tell us the desire of his heart, there's nothing that needs to be said here; everyone gets it. It's our society's collective sigh of wonderment, of angst-ridden youth, of the longing for something more. If Luke were a mermaid in a cartoon it would be his moment on the rock, thrusting his chin and chest out to the horizon, daring, wishing he were part of another world.

Maybe I was wrong and I was nothing like Luke Skywalker, and my childhood differed from Luke's in other substantial ways: he had robot friends, and screwy aliens as neighbors, or an ability to fly spaceships without any formal training. But I had those things, too, because like so many of us, they existed in my brain, in my shows, and in my books. Hey, what's Luke's favorite book anyway?

Sadly, Luke Skywalker doesn't have a favorite book. And even though he's the ultimate dreamer, a craver of adventure, a wide-eyed Joseph Campbell archetype hero, he's initially presented to us as kind of a philistine. This supposed pop descendant of Odysseus and Perseus lives in the zip code of a galaxy far, far away, meaning he's got no Shakespeare, Homer, Robert Louis Stevenson, J. M. Barrie, or even J. K. Rowling to get him excited about packing up and seeking adventure. In Star Wars, romantic notions of adventure don't spring from literature or a received tradition of storytelling. Instead, Luke wants to get out of the house and go to space because he's bored as fuck. And this boredom might not just be because Luke Skywalker doesn't have a favorite book; it's because he actually *can't* read.

As depicted in the first "real" *Star Wars* film, in 1977, Luke Skywalker—when you consider a substantial amount of evidence—is a functionally illiterate person, and his fellow citizens might not be much better off. Not once in any of the existing Star Wars movies does a person, droid, or creature pick up a book or newspaper, magazine, literary journal, or chapbook of Wookiee poetry. Instead, if something is briefly read by someone in Star Wars, it's like one sentence, read off a screen—and even then, almost certainly being "translated" by R2-D2. I say Luke and his buddies are *functionally* illiterate because this tiny amount of reading ends up being the difference between someone being fluent in a foreign language and having learned just enough to ask for directions. And any way you look at it, no one in Star Wars is reading for fun.

To be fair, finding a popular science fiction or fantasy universe richly populated with its own indigenous art—and more specifically, its own literature—is rare. The funnier-than-everyone novelist and book critic Lev Grossman once said to me, "No one reads any books in Narnia." Then, with the kind of shit-talking zeal that can only happen when one is bashing the things we love, Lev switched from C. S. Lewis to J. K. Rowling and explained to me that he felt like Harry Potter wasn't really his "kind of hero" either because Harry Potter didn't seem to be a reader. And he's right, because when you think about it, Harry's pal Hermione really digs reading, but her bookish tendencies are treated as an aberration in a world of magic and adventure. More frighteningly, Hermione's love of reading and Harry's and Ron's doltishness actually just mirror most high school clichés and accidently reinforce them. The bookworm kid living in our world who really loves and reads the Harry Potter books can probably *only* identify with Hermione. More broadly, Harry's nonreader status is totally par for this particularly illiterate course of fantastic heroes. But maybe it's not his fault. Maybe an overabundance of stimuli might be to blame. I mean, if you lived at Hogwarts or were roommates with Princess Leia or had a house in Narnia, it stands to reason the escapism reading provides might not be in high demand. Instead, in these kinds of narratives, books tend to be plot devices the characters use to solve problems rather than truly wonderful ends in themselves.

Now, like me, you're totally aware there's a reason why long scenes in novels or movies with characters turning pages and sighing haven't ever once been a thing. You can't depict your characters reading books and hope for a lot of excitement, particularly if they're only reading for pleasure. So, I'm not saying we should "see" characters sitting around and reading. But books and reading change us, make us smarter, and so it bugs me how main characters from big sci-fi or fantasy epics don't seem to really dig reading. The existence or even suggestion of these activities in certain made-up worlds is alarmingly low.

In *The Lord of the Rings*, Gandalf's reading comes in the form of scrolls and prophecies to figure out what the hell is going on. He's blowing a lot of dust off this shit, too, because it always seems like no one has taken up this kind of thing for a long, long time. Even here in Middle-Earth, a world born from the very literate linguist J. R. R. Tolkien, a place where books *do* exist, they're treated like something other people used to handle. And then—either in the novels or the films—Gandalf's reading of old legends and myths is more like a training montage from a Rocky movie than anything else. Reading powers, ON! Plus, the suggestion that *The Hobbit or There and Back Again* exists as some sort of real book (Bilbo's life story?) is borderline insulting to a real memoirist. Because no one seems to ever read anyway, Bilbo writing his life story comes across like a delusional hobbyist deciding he can write a memoir, even though he's never read one.

Still, I love the Hobbits, and the Middle-Earth people, because even though they all don't read as much as I'd like them to, it's clear they do *have* books, which in part is why they get hip to so much cool stuff so fast. Gandalf might be cramming with those old books and scrolls, but at least he knows what he's looking at.

Very popular science fiction does a little bit better here, with characters on both *Star Trek* and *Battlestar Galactica* being totally down with theatre, novels, and poetry. And even though both the 1978–79 and 2003 versions of *Battlestar Galactica* take place in a similar Star Wars–esque galaxy (they're searching for "Earth," so they've got to be far, far away), people from Caprica and the other colonies read all the time. They've got so many different kinds of literature, in fact, that President Roslin even likes trashy murder-mystery novels, ones Admiral Adama reads to her by her beside. True, a lot of this made-up literature in *Battlestar* comes across as a little forced, but the attempt to at least create it is in staggering contrast to the paperless Star Wars universe.

Star Trek, meanwhile, has people quoting from Shakespeare and Milton practically from its first aired moments. Furthermore, the first "real" (debatable) episode of the original *Star Trek*, "Where No Man Has Gone Before," boasts a scene in which Gary Mitchell quotes from "Nightingale Woman," a fictional poem written by someone from another planet, featuring this staggering couplet: *My love has wings / slender feathered things*.

The fact that this space-poem totally sucks isn't the point; it's simply that even a one-off character like Gary Mitchell in Star Trek is way more of a well-read person than pretty much anyone we ever meet in Star Wars. Sure, in *Star Trek II: The Wrath of Khan*, Spock gives Kirk Charles Dickens's *A Tale of*

Two Cities as a birthday present. It's totally clear from the dialogue that these guys aren't all that familiar with Dickens, and maybe Spock is trying to start a book club in which these guys will get caught up on the classics in between phasering interstellar assholes and saving idiotic planets. It's like this book gift is on the sly, because we all know Kirk and Spock both cut class in college and are undereducated, too. But still, it's cool these guys are trying.

In his 2009 nonfiction book, *The Tyranny of E-mail*, John Freeman talks a little about Star Trek, pointing out that "science fiction may not always predict the future, but it is often a brilliant counter-mythology—a visible cultural symptom—of our prevailing anxieties." Meaning if the best and brightest people in Star Trek are a little behind on reading, it seems like a pretty realistic possibility. I'm not sure if there are science fiction writers who live in the futuristic world of Star Trek— what could they possibly write about?*—but I do know that no one in the future-world of *The Hunger Games* has a desire to read, become a librarian, or write anything other than memoir. You could make an argument that Star Trek is a utopian vision of the future, and *The Hunger Games* is a dystopian one, but when it comes to how books are regarded, these two wildly different science fiction future-worlds are both downers, at least in relationship to the future of literacy. Being a writer is not a serious thing in these futures, and books are regarded as an

---

* I mean, I'd love to read a science fiction story from a science fiction author who lives inside of Star Trek. Who wouldn't? It's too bad H. G. Wells never wrote a science fiction story about a science fiction author living in the twenty-first century.

old-school curiosity. Science fiction isn't necessarily proud of its dystopian stance on the future of books, but the idea that people stop reading in the future often seems like a foregone conclusion. In fact, the entire plots of both *Zardoz* and *Logan's Run* end up hinging on the staggering amounts of ignorance most people have, with the former depicting a mustachioed Sean Connery going on a murderous rampage because he found a copy of Frank Baum's *The Wonderful Wizard of Oz* in an abandoned library. So, the extremely common sci-fi narrative about reading goes something like this: people get lazy, they forget to read, and everything goes to hell. Still, as bad as Katniss's education might be, like Kirk and Spock, and unlike Luke Skywalker, she can actually (probably) read.

Does Star Wars just not have time for all that crap? As epic fantasy, it's therefore not concerned with the specifics of what people are up to outside of the adventure. Here, realism and culture don't matter as much as story. Many people love to point out (often correctly, I might add) that the debate between science fiction and fantasy sort of permanently wages inside of Star Wars, insofar as science fiction often strives to be more realistic while fantasy is more whimsical and thematic. And yet, there are technical rules about the Force in Star Wars, just as magic has rules in Harry Potter, *The Lord of the Rings*, and Narnia. Plus, in science fiction or fantasy, a fictional "world" has to make sense in order for us to buy the plot, no matter how brass-tacks plausible and whimsically thematic it might be.

But this isn't about calling out the culture of Star Wars as unrealistic. Nope. I'm actually saying the opposite. It's totally realistic. In fact, it's the lack of reading and books that helps explain why this fictional culture is so screwed up and oppressed. Our media says a lot about us, and in the case of the culture of Star Wars, its indigenous media speaks volumes. In the Star Wars films there is utterly no reportage or journalism, which actually starts to make the possibility of widespread illiteracy more and more likely. In the prequel films—where a more democratic government is supposedly intact—there is a black hole of political news. In *The Phantom Menace* we see floating little cameras bobbing around Natalie Portman in the Senate, but these cameras don't seem to be actually feeding this information anywhere. After watching all the Star Wars movies, we'll later figure out these cameras aren't news cameras and they're just for security.* This gets weirder when you realize that Natalie Portman is only there to talk to the Senate *in person* to plead her case because, presumably, no reputable news outlet has *written* about the blockade/invasion of her entire planet.

In the next two *Star Wars* prequels, we're fairly clued in to the idea that the government is mostly manipulated by Palpatine, and as such, everything related to the Senate seems to be all about systematically curtailing basic rights and screwing up democratic mojo. But in *The Phantom Menace*, right at the purported start of the saga, before Palps takes over and becomes a liberty-hating zap-faced monster, it looks like we're already

---

* In *Revenge of the Sith*, we find out these kinds of "security" recordings are mostly just of unspeakable acts of horror, which Ewan McGregor watches after the fact. Who would presumably be watching security feeds at the Galactic Senate or the Jedi Temple anyway? Rent-a-cops with low-yield lightsabers? What's the Star Wars version of a Taser?

dealing with a closed, secretive government. Because if you get rid of journalists, it seems like you wouldn't even need the Dark Side of the Force to manipulate everyone. Samuel L. Jackson and Yoda sit around and talk a lot in these movies about how "the Dark Side clouds everything," but I think what they're alluding to might just be a giant information gap, one which could be filled by a newspaper.

"But wait!" you might be saying again. "People in Star Wars can totally read!" This is because you, like me, maybe love these films and, as such, totally know for a FACT that there are scenes in which R2-D2 sends little messages for Luke to read on his screen. There's writing on the tractor-beam controls, too, and people in the ships are looking at buttons with letters on them. We've got to talk about this. And we've got to talk about Aurebesh, which—as somewhere, right now, a hard-core fan is saying out loud at the top of his or her lungs—is the "official" language of Star Wars.

Aurebesh, like most things involved with explaining Star Wars, is a retroactive invention, and it certainly wasn't created by George Lucas. In the original version of *A New Hope*, the tractor-beam controls that Obi-Wan tampers with have the English words "tractor beam" printed underneath them. But in the 1997 restored special edition (and technically canonical version) of the film, "tractor beam" has been replaced by characters that, according to many, are letters in the Aurebesh alphabet. Indeed, in the trailer for the brand-new Star Wars film—*The Force Awakens*—we see a pilot with writing on his flight suit, which hard-core fans have "confirmed" is Aurebesh, and the words, when translated, say "pull to inflate."

Here's the thing, though—Aurebesh was created by one person: John Hazlett. He wrote for a variety of manuals that tied in with the Star Wars role-playing games in the 1990s and later authored an article for the official Star Wars website called "The Written Word," which outlines the existence and origins of Aurebesh. He did a lot of writing and research in between and successfully produced a near-academic-level analysis of where written words and languages show up in Star Wars. He's also only one person, and the majority of his research relies heavily on the texts from Star Wars novels, comics, and, of course, games.

Ironically or not, here on our planet, there are probably more hours devoted to the reading of Star Wars books than the watching of the Star Wars movies. In the pages of many of these stories, you may believe that you've found evidence that directly contradicts my theory of functional illiteracy. But then again, these books and comics also contradict each other about a whole lot of stuff, including what Jabba the Hutt looks like, what Luke Skywalker's mom's name really was (not Natalie Portman!), and whether or not anyone is allowed to have a pink lightsaber. But it doesn't really matter. Because let's say Hazlett is right. Let's say Aurebesh is the predominant written language in the Star Wars galaxy. Let's say there's a long, detailed historical account of how it came to be. Let's say the vast majority of his research (half of which created itself, but whatever) is correct. It still doesn't mean that I'm wrong about functional illiteracy. I'm not denying there wasn't a written language in this fictional galaxy at some point; I'm simply asserting that the evidence seems to indicate most people aren't reading, and I think that's because they can't, or because their reading comprehension is very limited.

Even in cases of limited reading, the "letters" (maybe Aurebesh) and pieces of writing are *directly* related to *tasks*. Pilots for the Empire (or the Clones for the Republic) are probably functionally literate, because they go through some kind of training academy. However, I think the larger sample evidence we get suggests a culture much more reliant on technology and droids than you might think. Luke's ability to read a little bit of droid-speak (again, maybe Aurebesh) from a screen is, as I mentioned, totally analogous to people who learn just enough of a foreign language to get by. The person in control of this exchange, the one putting up with Luke's crappy reading skills, is R2-D2. The overall literacy and education in Star Wars is very catch-as-catch-can. Han can understand Chewbacca because he *needs* to. Luke figures out how to fly spaceships from racing T-16s through Beggar's Canyon. Anakin intuits how to build both a podracer and C-3PO as a little kid because he's fucking magic. Everything awesome that anyone does in Star Wars is slop, with only the most exceptional characters accidentally getting enough of a spark of information to become epically heroic (i.e., the Rebels or the Jedi). And the people they're liberating are ignorant and disenfranchised as a result in generations and generations of illiteracy and decline in information exchange. We don't need to go too far out of the Skywalker family for proof either.

In *A New Hope*, Uncle Owen needs a droid who can speak bocce and then says something about the binary language of his moisture vaporators. Right here we've got our whole

microcosm of how this illiteracy actually exists and functionally perpetuates itself: Uncle Owen needs a translator, and
more specifically, needs one machine that can talk to another
machine, so he can do his job. This doesn't sound like a guy
who has gotten a suitable education, but rather one who uses
droids and computers to Google things that he should kind of
just already know. Sure, having droids talk in computer code to
each other isn't something any human can really do, but can
Uncle Owen do anything without a robot? Maybe if he read
some books he could fix his marriage.

In a way, Star Wars presents a way we'd all get by if widespread illiteracy actually became a fact of life. In our own culture, pictograms and emojis often replace words on traffic signs,
on restroom doors, in texts, etc. The buttons being pressed by
the Death Star control-room workers might not even be letters at
all. They might be pictograms representing different functions,
functions like "death ray blast" and "trash compact." Plus, how
could those guys read anything in those helmets anyway?

This isn't to say there isn't an elite class of people who can
read. The more educated people like the Jedi Knights can probably read, and maybe even write. But their record-keeping systems seem to be obscenely reliant on video-style data rather
than text. In *Attack of the Clones* Obi-Wan Kenobi goes to the
Jedi Library, but this research facility seems less about books
and more about pretty colors, interactive holographic maps,
etc. Obi-Wan basically walks into the library and asks for the
interactive games rather than the books. Even a character as
wise and supposedly awesome as Obi-Wan Kenobi doesn't do
all that much reading, at least that we see.

One invention of the expanded universe—specifically the Dark Horse Comics—was the idea that ancient Jedi Knights recorded their stuff in little holograms called "holocrons." This adds another piece of evidence in the history of Star Wars functional illiteracy because it seems to prove that a switch from written communication to visual and audio media has been under way for a long, long time in this galaxy. The predilection of the Jedi to have a bias against reading for pleasure can be found in the pages of the comic series *Tales of the Jedi: The Golden Age of the Sith*. Here, supposedly some five thousand years before "real" Star Wars, a quirky little alien Jedi Knight named Odan-Urr is really digging on reading "old" scrolls and "ancient records," and gets chastised by his Jedi master, who says, "You would be content to spend your life in the company of scrolls and documents . . . but a Jedi Knight has other responsibilities. Other duties." Like I said, there was a written language, and written documents, but through bias or new technology, the tendency to rely on this media went away. Humans and aliens populating their universe used the written word for the purposes of getting their basic culture off the ground—for commerce only—and as soon as holograms were available, switched over. If we use the basic reductive interpretation of Marshall McLuhan's axiom "the medium is the message," then the medium of Jedi holocrons seems to send a message that recorded verbal information is preferable to the craft of writing.

Still, let's just assume Jedi can probably read and are taught to read, as are rich people like Princess Leia, Padmé Amidala, and Jimmy Smits. But everything, everything, everything in

Star Wars is about video chat via holograms or verbal communication through com-links. Of course, for these cultures to have progressed and become space-faring entities, they needed written language at some point. But when we catch up to the "now" of Star Wars, the necessity to actually learn to read and write has all but faded away. We can then imagine a social class of educated readers, possibly engineers and programmers, who know how to build and repair translators and computers, and droids. These people likely have awesome jobs, and everyone else is sort of screwed. There's a lot of poverty in Star Wars, and it seems like it's totally connected to widespread ignorance.

The idea of education becoming obsolete due to cultural changes was a science fiction precedent, straight from Star Wars' main competitor: Star Trek. In the first Star Trek thing *ever*, "The Cage," Vina speaks of a culture that "forgets how to repair the machines left behind by their ancestors." This is what I think happened with literacy in the Star Wars galaxy. People stopped using the written word all that much because they didn't need to, and it slipped away from being a commonly held skill. If somebody writes "tractor beam" in Aurebesh on a control panel, but most people don't know what it says, does it really count?

Between the end of the prequels (*Revenge of the Sith*) and the beginning of the classic films (*A New Hope*), only nineteen years pass. This means the existence of the literate Jedi Knights mutates from a fact of everyday life into legend, seemingly overnight. (We've seen this in the new cartoon show *Rebels*, where being a Jedi is something you conceal to avoid persecution.) Even one of Vader's cronies calls the Force an "ancient religion," which a joyless, cynical fan could easily dismiss as one of the many oft-pointed-out continuity problems between the prequels and the originals. But if we pretend like all of this is gospel and it does work, then the hyperbolic rendering of the Jedi/the Force into "ancient" might not be so far-fetched when we consider very few people read or are informed at all about, really, anything at all. Because the average citizen of the galaxy in Star Wars receives his/her/its information orally, from stories told by spacers in bars, farm boys on arid planets, orphans in crime-ridden cities, etc., any kind of outrageous claim seems possible. These days, on Earth, a game of telephone can quickly spread nonfacts via social media. Star Wars has this game of telephone without the reading. When Palpatine ominously takes over the government in *Revenge of the Sith* by raising his arms like he's Tom Petty at a concert playing "Learning to Fly," everyone goes along with him, because he's an influencer. Palpatine verbally tweets "The Jedi tried to kill me" and everyone is like "Wow, bummer." And it's not just because they're too lazy to read the original documents: there aren't any, and even if there were, they couldn't. In this scene, Natalie Portman points out that liberty dies "with thunderous applause," but really their liberty is dying because most of them are powerless and disenfranchised. Most of the surviving characters at the end of the prequels are the bad guys, and they can probably read. And if the Jedi seem to be the most educated people in the prequels, that all changes when they are systematically murdered. The easy analogy would be a real-life government going and burning down all the colleges and schools and killing all the teachers, but the information manipulation seems more important here. If you have evil intentions, once books are gone, you're in good shape. But killing the only people who could have read them? Even better. Maybe Natalie Portman should have said "This is how *literacy* dies . . ."

Weirdly or not, the God-Papa of Star Wars—George Lucas—actually intended for this to be a "paperless universe." In numerous pre-1997 books and interviews, Lucas mentions the fact that he wanted his worlds to be devoid of paper, which, far from taking credit away from him, actually seems to indicate all of this illiteracy is at least indirectly intentional.* We don't need to hate on George Lucas to prove most of his protagonists can't read, and in fact, it's possible he wouldn't disagree with this interpretation (though he'd probably be super-annoyed with this much analytical zeal). George Lucas is obviously an extremely literate dude and famously (or infamously, depending on one's mood) based much of the mythological archetype action in Star Wars on Joseph Campbell's *Hero with a Thousand Faces*, meaning the "message" of Star Wars is clearly individuality, creativity, freedom, and everything else that seems to be a positive way to think about a society. And yet, I can't help but feel with all of its psychological influence on our culture, Star Wars was accidentally prescient in its telegraphing of the eventual result of a less and less literate society. If you're reading the *Wikipedia* entry about a novel, *instead of reading a novel*, or

---

* You might ask: how could someone be "indirectly intentional"? George Lucas once wore a shirt to the set of *Indiana Jones IV* that said "Han Shot First." George Lucas is the person who changed it so Han didn't shoot first. He's like this all the time; does something that doesn't make sense and then retroactively makes "sense" of it.

you're getting bent out of shape about a friend's tweet about social injustice, without really *knowing what they're talking about*, I'd say we're only a few centuries away from someone building a Death Star in secret and a whole populace randomly accepting the mass genocide of smarty-pants wizards. Yoda tells us the path to the Dark Side includes anger, fear, and aggression, but I think he forgot to mention ignorance.

Dramatically, I think it is very dope that Obi-Wan puts a lightsaber in Luke's hand, but if he wanted to prevent all of this, then he and Qui-Gon Jinn should have been going around teaching people on poor planets to read years and years prior. In a meta-criticism of the universe he actually lives in, Han Solo says, "Hokey religions and ancient weapons are no match for a good blaster at your side." If we read "hokey religions and ancient weapons" as a stand-in for "Star Wars," then we can also pretend that "blasters" become "books." If there are to be real Skywalkers in our world—those who swoop in to save a decadent and dulling culture from dangerous laziness—complete with wide-eyed idealism and string sections in our guts, you can bet we'll all be just a little bit, maybe a lot bit, better read.

Wearing Dracula's Pants

Say what you will about hipsters and the twenty-first-century epidemic of skinny jeans, but as a teenager growing up in the '90s, I was glad to get a reprieve from the super-baggy-can't-touch-this pants options of the previous decade. Though, to be honest, when I started buying and wearing pants that were a little tighter, it probably had less to do with being a hipster and more to do with trying to be like Dracula.*

In the 1931 film adaptation of *Dracula*, Bela Lugosi's history-making turn as the famous vampire finds the character with superpowers coming out of his ears: he can transform into bats and wolves (the latter, offscreen), he can fly, be invisible (also offscreen, for obvious reasons), suck your blood, control your mind, and make an impressive real estate negotiation in which he swaps a castle in Transylvania for one in England. But his most lasting superpower is easily his sense of style. No

---

* Who is probably a hipster, too.

one else in this movie looks nearly as suave as Lugosi's Dracula, and in a contest between who has the better pants—Dracula versus the movie's "good guy," John Harker—Dracula totally wins.

Monster-guru John Landis told me once that he thought because of the "exchange of bodily fluids," vampires were always about sex.* He also said that Lugosi's portrayal of the character redefined how we thought about Dracula: "In the book he's not sexy," Landis said, "but Bela Lugosi was this hot matinee idol in Budapest. What is considered stilted acting now was quite dashing then."

Because vampires have been connected with sex since forever, Lugosi's decision to play Dracula as a slick, overtly sexual, fashion-forward icon isn't without its literary roots. Predating the 1897 Bram Stoker novel by seventy-eight years, John William Polidori's 1819 short story "The Vampyre" featured a smooth operator named Lord Ruthven, a suave, sexy vampire who gives Dorian Gray a foppish and vapid run for his money. Written during a super-famous dark and stormy night while hanging out with Mary Shelley, Percy Shelley, and Lord Byron, this short story is often credited with giving everybody the idea that immortal people who drink your blood will also be people you'll want to sleep with.

Considerably less sexy than Lord Ruthven is James Malcolm Rymer's 1845 vampire, Varney, who stars in the serialized

---

* John Landis has directed a lot of great horror flicks, but people like me really only know him as the guy who directed Michael Jackson's "Thriller." The chances of you being a person like me on this particular thing are probably higher than with anything else I'll claim in my whole life.

"novel" *Varney the Vampire, or The Feast of Blood*. This multi-part thingamabob was part of those "penny dreadfuls" you've probably heard about: cheap publications in Victorian England that were designed to elicit thrills from readers and to get them coming back for the next installment. If you were to time-travel back to the 1840s and try to simulate bad television through prose, *Varney the Vampire* would probably be what you would come up with, and you'd be a genius for doing it. It's thin on characters and consistency, but heavy on engaging the reader with exclamation points and weird, bizarrely direct questions. Asking "What is that—a strange, pattering noise, as of a million of fairy feet?" or "Was that lightning?" the sentences themselves do almost everything short of saying, "Do you see the Vampire?" Calling the writing clunky would be too easy and a tad cruel, but there does seem to be something of the proto–Choose Your Own Adventure book imbedded in penny dreadfuls, plus there are a lot of other cool vampire-firsts in *Varney*. The whole look-into-my-eyes mind-control thing originates here, as do the fangs that leave the telltale two-pronged vamp-nip on the neck. Neither Lord Ruthven nor Varney had to be invited to your house to start terrorizing people, but Varney is decidedly grosser in appearance than Lord Ruthven, meaning Varney took some sexy points away from vampires for a while.

A few decades later, things heat up again. Twenty-six years before the novel *Dracula*, in 1871, Irishman Joseph Thomas Sheridan Le Fanu drops his novella "Carmilla," which gives us the first lesbian vampires. Although Carmilla is more adept at seduction than Varney, even the reader isn't totally sure who or what she is at first. Most important, and unlike those dumb male vampires before her, she becomes the first vampire who really has to be invited inside your house in order to bite you.* In 1897, Bram Stoker's Dracula also has to be invited in, and Stoker borrows even more from "Carmilla" than just that! Stoker has Dracula turning into a dog in the novel, and Carmilla turns into a black cat. Both Dracula and Carmilla have a propensity to only strike at nighttime, and in "Carmilla," there's even a vampire-hunting expert named Baron Vordenburg whose name doesn't sound at all like that of Dracula's nemesis, Dr. Van Helsing.† Both Vordenburg and Van Helsing are Dutch persons, and yet, the American phrase "going Dutch" for some reason never caught on to mean "locating and killing vampires." We live in a screwed-up world.

So, how did we get sexy vampires from all of this stuff? Isn't this Bram Stoker guy's novel *Dracula* an unsexy giant rip-off of a bunch of other vampire stories that came before it? Kind of,

---

* There's some debate on this qualifying as the first printed "vampire invitation," but because "Carmilla" directly influenced Stoker's *Dracula*, I say it counts.

† This character has been played by a lot of actors over the years, including Laurence Olivier, Anthony Hopkins, and Peter Fonda. Peter Cushing, who is probably most famous for being Darth Vader's friend—Grand Moff Tarkin—in the original *Star Wars*, practically made his whole career with this role, starring opposite Christopher Lee's Dracula. Christopher Plummer and David Warner have also played Van Helsing and both of those dudes were Klingons in the same Star Trek movie, 1991's *The Undiscovered Country*. In the 1931 *Dracula,* Van Helsing was played by a guy named Edward Van Sloan, who was also in 1931's *Frankenstein* and 1932's *The Mummy,* where he basically played the exact same character: older concerned man with all the answers. But really, truly, never forget Van Helsing was played by HUGH JACKMAN in the 2004 crapfest movie *Van Helsing.* Still, even with all these famous people having played Van Helsing, I just can't picture any actor saying, "Wow, what a great character."

but *Dracula* had some loose historical basis, too. Most people who dig vampires agree that Stoker based Dracula's background on a fifteenth-century Bulgarian folk hero named Vlad the Impaler,* sometimes called Vlad Dracula, but never Vlad "the Butch."† The novel also sports cool narrative flips and was widely praised by Stoker's contemporaries, including Sherlock Holmes creator Sir Arthur Conan Doyle. It was more loved than *any other* vampire thing before, maybe because it just happened to be a full-blown, whole novel. So, rip-off or skilled literary mash-up, *Dracula* brought vampires into the twentieth century, and the character himself became *the* vampire to beat.

This isn't to say he'll always be that way. To put it in perspective, if you were to ask somebody twenty years ago to name the "most famous" fictional novel about wizards, people would probably say J. R. R. Tolkien's *The Lord of the Rings*. Today, I'm sure Tolkien would get mentioned for sure, but I bet more people would say J. K. Rowling's Harry Potter books. And then you'd suddenly realize only forty-two years passed between J. R. R. Tolkien publishing *The Return of the King* in 1955 and J. K. Rowling putting out the first Harry Potter novel in 1997. After just four decades, Rowling's wizards are arguably way more recognizable in the pop zeitgeist than Tolkien's wizards. On the vampire front: it was fifty-two years between Varney

---

* The 2014 movie *Dracula Untold* tried to take the Vlad angle more seriously. It wasn't awful.

† In *Ghostbusters II*, the main antagonist is the spirit of a fifteenth-century sorcerer named Vigo the Carpathian. He's given a lot of names, including Vigo the Unholy and Vigo the Despised. Bill Murray adds "Vigo the Butch." Vigo's backstory is totally a Dracula homage.

and Dracula, and Stoker almost permanently took over vampire fiction until Anne Rice started up. The average person probably thinks of Dracula as being the "original" vampire, even though he isn't, and even he's hanging on by a thread these days. So, it's not inconceivable that in one hundred years Harry Potter or Dumbledore could be considered the "original" wizards, not Merlin or Gandalf. Who knows who the twenty-second century's big vampire will be? Maybe Edward Cullen?

But why do we still care? And how is it connected with sex? When we consider the very real fact that at least half of the people who claim to like vampires have never even read *Dracula*, how do we account for everyone's total and complete familiarity and obsession with him? Not only has everyone heard of Dracula, they can literally *hear his voice* in their brains, just like the "real" Dracula if he were controlling your mind. I'm talking of course about the *"I vant to suck your blouud"* Transylvania accent.

A few Octobers ago, I went to one of these haunted corn mazes the week before Halloween. It was in Sleepy Hollow, New York, and after watching a little nifty Headless Horseman show, my girlfriend and I lined up for the entrance to the maze. Suddenly, a faux-Transylvanian accent came booming out of the loudspeakers: *"Gouood evening . . . and velcome to the horrors that avait you in the maze beyond . . ."* I looked around and quickly found on a raised platform the master of ceremonies, a teenage kid in half-assed Beetlejuice makeup wearing a mic that was part of a headset, like she was Shakira or a telemarketer. Playing this "character" was probably going to help her get her equity card. I was so pissed, and not just because the accent was bad, but because it was so out of place with the Sleepy Hollow stuff. "It's not even period specific," I hissed under my breath. My girlfriend rolled her eyes. It's a wonder why anyone hangs out with me at all.

Still, it's weird that some poor, struggling actor working a crummy haunted maze in upstate New York inherently just *knows* to put on the Dracula voice if she needs a bargain-basement "Halloween voice." It's not like this kid did an impression of Kristen Stewart as Bella Swan or David Boreanaz from *Buffy the Vampire Slayer*. Most people still associate the word "vampire" with Dracula. And even though *Sesame Street*'s Count has a lot to do with that, I'm not convinced that's the only reason. What I'm saying is this: even if people *don't* think of Bela Lugosi *specifically* when they hear that "scary voice," it's still the go-to scary voice because it started out not as a scary voice but instead as an I'm-trying-to-seduce-you voice.

If it's possible to get blasphemous about the unholy, I'm going to go ahead and say what I've been dancing around: Dracula the literary character *is not super interesting*, but Dracula the cinematic character as played by Bela Lugosi is. This sexed-up, over-the-top performance from Bela Lugosi is what saved the whole thing from obscurity. The character in the book spoke with perfect English, but that doesn't really work in a movie. So, in the approximation of the thing, the simulacrum of Dracula becomes the "real Dracula."

If you're a film snob, you're probably blowing a gasket now and asserting that the 1922 German film *Nosferatu* is a more important vampire movie than 1931's *Dracula*, but I call arty bullshit on that. *Nosferatu* was an unauthorized "retelling" of the Stoker novel, and it's not funny, and it's certainly not sexy. It might take vampires more seriously than the Lugosi film, and might be true to the creepy spirit of the novel, but to me, all of that doesn't make it legit. Actually, to get rowdy for a second, *Nosferatu* is a snobby idea of what a vampire movie should be: obscure, hard to watch, off-putting. I admit that it might legitimately be a better piece of art than the 1931 *Dracula*, but it's not a movie I'd rather watch. Lugosi is just *cooler*.

In the Lugosi movie, when Dracula moves from Transylvania to London, the first thing he does is crash the opera and start making the moves on the ladies. In particular he's interested in Miss Mina (Helen Chandler), though Mina's friend Miss Lucy (Frances Dade) has the hots for Dracula just a little bit more. Soon after Dracula chats them up, the women are combing their hair and gossiping about how great Dracula is. Mina mentions she wants someone more "normal," to which Lucy dismissively says, "Like John?" As I alluded to before, John Harker (David Manners) does not wear cool pants. He's practically swimming in his giant I-go-to-the-country-club pants, and Manners plays the white-bread-boy character with unintentional schmaltz. John isn't nearly as cool or interesting as Dracula. This guy is a bro of the same ilk as Jack Driscoll from *King Kong*, and I love imagining a spin-off movie where the two of them play flip-cup and argue about fantasy football or if their girlfriends are ever allowed to be alone. If John were absent in *Dracula*, it would free up the movie from having to be saddled with a traditional hero, and then maybe Dracula would win! There's a great scene toward the end when Mina—partially under Dracula's power—tells John that "it's all over." The finality of her tone has the shadow of a real breakup, and for a second you get the notion that Mina actually *wants* to be with Dracula, and this isn't mind control at all.

If you're wondering why monsters like Dracula have such power over us in general, it's right here in this movie. Both Mina and Lucy were into Dracula arguably before he started using mind-powers, and even if they weren't, we—the audience— totally were. Dracula is either the bad boy we want to become or the taboo bad boy we might want to date. Bela Lugosi embodied the best taboo aspects of vampires, which started with Lord Ruthven and, of course, Carmilla. If the vampire is "the biter," then post-Carmilla, and the cinematic 1931 *Dracula*, "the bitee" becomes complicit in the whole thing. We're literally rooting for Dracula to win. These jokers he's hanging out with aren't ready for his sense of style or his crazy ideas about relationships. Lugosi's Dracula is the sexy monster, the thing we wish we could either possess or become, if regular boring life weren't standing in the way.

Another iconic vampire—Barnabas Collins (Jonathan Frid) from the long-running soap opera *Dark Shadows**—is similarly loved by audiences (and other characters) without having to rely on vampire mind-control powers. In 2013, I was lucky enough to talk to Joseph Caldwell,† one of the original writers

---

* *Dark Shadows*, created by Dan Curtis, ran from 1966 to 1971 on ABC. It aired five nights a week. Its cult following is the definition of "cult following."

† Joe Caldwell is one of the nicest people I've ever met. Because of the way the *Dark Shadows* writers' room worked, Caldwell doesn't have a lot of official credit for the writing of some of the Barnabas story lines. But he also won the Rome Prize for literature, so I really doubt he's lying about the *Dark Shadows* stuff.

of *Dark Shadows*. He told me that contextualizing Barnabas as a sympathetic vampire was essential to prevent the character from just being seen as a "serial killer." Caldwell explained that a vampire's urge to kill is a "compulsion" and likened it (as Landis did) to a sexual act. "It's a metaphor for compulsive sex!" Caldwell declared, and he was probably right. The ratings for *Dark Shadows* reportedly went up to twenty million viewers after the introduction of Barnabas Collins.* And the reason why all those people rooted for Barnabas to "win" had nothing to do with him having powers over people or possessing them, but instead, because Caldwell and other writers played the character straight. If the audience didn't buy Barnabas Collins as a real person, they wouldn't care. Which is the same reason why Dracula beat out Varney, both on the page and, of course, as Lugosi. In fact, the *Dark Shadows* writers' room was so in love with the 1931 *Dracula* that Caldwell claims the writers often intentionally mangled the warm Italian salutation "Tante Bella Cose"† to become "Tante Bela Lugosi!"

Other non-vampire monster movies often take their cues from *Dracula*, specifically 1933's *King Kong*. We're told by that movie's metafictional filmmaker Carl Denham that we're watching a "Beauty and the Beast" story, but that's too simple. Faye Wray's Ann Darrow in *King Kong* has way less agency

---

* Most people assume *Dark Shadows* was always about the vampire Barnabas. But it's not true. He wasn't introduced until Episode 211, when Dan Curtis asked Caldwell and others to cook up the vampire story. The character was supposed to be part of a temporary story arc. If you want, you can call this the "Urkel effect," since '90s sitcom *Family Matters* has a similar issue; supposedly, reoccurring uber-nerd Steve Urkel (Jaleel White) was so popular snapping his suspenders that he was made a regular.

† Roughly translates from Italian as "wishing you all the beautiful things."

than Miss Mina in *Dracula*. The real reason Denham calls the King Kong story "Beauty and the Beast" is because he's a flim-flam man, trying to sell everyone on the idea that Ann Darrow might have learned to love Kong. And unlike Dracula, she doesn't really. And could you blame her? What could they have in common?

The more a monster looks like a grotesque inhuman crea-ture, the more the metaphor becomes uninteresting. In 1954's *Creature from the Black Lagoon*, there are *two* men—not count-ing the titular creature—who are vying for the affections of the leading lady, Kay. One is the supposed nice guy, David, and the other, Mark, is a big-time asshole. In these kinds of movies, we can often tell which guy is a huge jerk because he'll be the one more willing to use violence against whoever the monster in the movie happens to be. Because we're already kind of root-ing for the monster in these situations (you get 'em, Dracula/King Kong/Creature!), siding against the monstrous human male who is foaming at the mouth for bloodshed becomes easy.

Even the original *Godzilla* (*Gojira* in Japan) wasn't immune to this formula. Never, never forget: a major plot point in the classic first ever *Godzilla* is the fact that young, handsome boat captain Hideto Ogata and his girlfriend, Emiko, jointly decide to put their engagement announcement on hold because, duh, Godzilla is attacking! If monsters existed in real life, psycholo-gists would probably see a pattern in people trying to weasel out of committed relationships because they're afraid of "Drac-ula" or "King Kong" or "Godzilla." Which is just a metaphor for a commitment-phobic person. In the newest 2014 incarna-tion of *Godzilla*, the screenwriters are either completely aware of this monster-as-home-wrecker theme, or are totally unaware. Either way, the effect is the same. The new Godzilla doesn't threaten the romances of any of the movie's human characters, really, but instead, we're told he's only put on this Earth to stop OTHER monsters from having sex. Godzilla in the twenty-first century is a thing that monster-blocks his fellow monsters.

If your relationship can survive monsters, I suppose it's a strong one, and that, maybe more than anything, is why we love monsters so much. We go on dates to scary movies or to haunted houses to grab on to each other and test the ability that we can get through something as frightening as a vampire or huge ape. Dating someone who doesn't like scary movies or haunted houses is fine, but you should still probably watch one with someone you love anyway, just to make sure you can both survive it. Part of why jerky guys like John in *Dracula* are so lame is their total disbelief in the existence of this far-out stuff in the first place. The idea there could even be a vampire, another way of living your life, another place to buy your pants, is just totally out of the possibilities of this character's mental and emotional universe. Which is why, while watching the movie (or reading the book), we hate those characters, and we want them to get what is coming to them.

One of the smartest monster movies of all time, and one of the few classics that doesn't pit boring nice guys against sexy, exciting monsters is the excellent 1941 flick *The Wolf-Man*. Instead of monster versus boring guy, both things are made into the same character. Lon Chaney Jr. plays Larry Talbot, a dough-faced, totally likable, not conventionally handsome guy-next-door. Early on in the movie, Talbot is bitten by a gypsy named Bela, who—you're never going to believe it—is played by BELA LUGOSI. That's right, Dracula himself passes the monster fangs to the new monster in this movie. This is kind of like when Richard Roundtree shows up in the 2002 remake of *Shaft* to give Samuel L. Jackson's new Shaft advice about being Shaft.

In terms of its relationship to source material, 1941's *The Wolf-Man* doesn't have quite the same literary lineage as 1931's *Dracula*. Though there was Alexandre Dumas's 1857 story "The Wolf Leader," and an earlier 1831 story "The Man-Wolf," by Leitch Ritchie, neither is a canonical work that really defines how werewolves behave in future pop-werewolf narratives. In fact, there's really one true Victorian novel about werewolves, released one year before *Dracula*, 1896's *The Were-Wolf*, written by suffrage legend Clemence Annie Houseman. Like "Carmilla," *The Were-Wolf* can be seen as an early feminist work, featuring female werewolves devouring men who mean to destroy them. Unlike "Carmilla," it was, thankfully, written by a woman, and influenced horror writers like H. P. Lovecraft probably more than the novel *Dracula*.

The year 1933 saw the publication of the Guy Endore novel *A Werewolf of Paris*, and though it was a *New York Times* number one best seller that year, it was not at all associated with the first two black-and-white Universal Pictures werewolf movies. Prior to 1941's *The Wolf-Man*, Universal had put out a movie called *Werewolf of London*, which you'd think would be *A Werewolf of Paris*, only in London, but it's not. Instead, *Werewolf of*

London is more like a remake of *The Strange Case of Dr. Jekyll and Mr. Hyde*, a Robert Louis Stevenson novel you might have heard of, which, if you squint, is a quasi-werewolf story, too. The notion of a split personality, of being one thing one moment and being something else in another, is, at least in most versions, part of what werewolf stories are all about. With its mad scientist and potions, *Dr. Jekyll and Mr. Hyde* is bona fide science fiction; what if chemistry and *not magic* could turn a person into a monster? Sir Arthur Conan Doyle plays with the exact same idea in the 1922 Sherlock Holmes story "The Creeping Man,"* in which an old geezer named Professor Presbury injects himself with monkey testosterone in order to become younger, but accidentally just starts acting like a monkey.

For me, a weekend, full-moon monster is markedly different than an I'm-a-monster-all-the-time thing like Dracula. The biggest difference between Dr. Jekyll and the Wolf-Man is that the Wolf-Man—as represented by Lon Chaney Jr.'s Larry Talbot—didn't ask to be bitten. Instead, this sort of monster is a regular person who *becomes* a monster; and through biting, the conversion from a regular person to a monster is shared by both vampire fiction and werewolf fiction. The difference with the latter is that werewolves seem to contain the monsters inside of them, which, instead of having a deranged outside reason for your relationship not working out, actually turns that monster–home-wrecker thing back on you. See, it's not the monster's fault you can't commit to a date; it's yours.

* See more in "Baker Streets on Infinite Earths."

Larry Talbot wants to have a nice relationship with Gwen in *The Wolf-Man*, but unlike King Kong snatching Ann Darrow away from Jack, or Dracula brainwashing Miss Mina to screw over John, Larry has only himself to blame when his particular relationship doesn't work out. If we have sympathy for Larry as he's beaten to death by his dad in the final scene of *The Wolf-Man*, it makes sense, but what we're rooting for in this movie is a little more confusing than with *Dracula*. The Wolf-Man isn't cool, nor is he suave. In human form, Larry mumbles and embarrasses himself while flirting with Gwen. And as the Wolf-Man, he's not hypnotizing anyone with his ghoulish charm; he's just a fucking really scary wolf. And unlike Bela Lugosi, his pants are baggy and lame.

Lugosi gave us cool monsters in the '30s when he told us to listen to "the children of the night" and took them away in the '40s when he bit poor Larry Talbot. He changed the way we think about monsters, twice, in the blink of a cultural eye. First, he made monsters dashing, and something we wanted to root for and, perhaps, go to bed with. And then, when passing monsters to a new generation, he turned them into our worst fears: outrageously hairy people who can't control themselves, who can't commit to a relationship, and who also have no sense of style whatsoever. You know, real monsters.

The Sounds of Science Fiction

My mother didn't really believe me, but this was the album I wanted.

"You understand what the word 'symphony' means, right?"

I said that I did, even though I didn't. Being into science fiction when you're eleven often means you assume new words are actually just sci-fi things. I'm confident that watching Star Trek and reading science fiction and fantasy novels improved my vocabulary, but I'm not totally confident that the line between vocabulary words for real things and for fake ones was ever made all that clear. Rudimentarily, a lot of kids learn the word "dragon" or "unicorn" or "dinosaur" around the same time as "horse," "dog," and "barn," but understanding the difference between words for make-believe and words for real things is tough when make-believe is such a big part of the inner workings of your child brain.

If you've ever read a really good alternate-universe novel like China Mieville's *The City and the City* or anything by Paul

Park or the challenging dystopian jam *A Clockwork Orange*, then you know how this goes. You have to put in place-holder "blanks" for words you don't really get. I think because of the hardwiring of sci-fi to myself as a child, I still deal with unknown words and concepts in the same way one might read *A Clockwork Orange*, minus the glossary.

"Symphony," my mother said, seeing through my lie, "means there aren't any words, and this tape is just going to be lots of instruments playing the music from the movies." She made it sound like I wanted to buy one of those tapes that just had whale sounds on it. She didn't get it. But I was relieved and bobbed my head up and down excitedly. By questioning the whole "symphony" thing, she'd had me worried for a second; maybe this excellent cassette tape I'd spotted in Sam Goody wasn't what I wanted at all. But it was. This was the soundtrack to a better, more adventurous world. Yes. This is what I wanted.

The tape was *Star Trek: The Astral Symphony*, a 1991 release that was a "greatest hits" collection featuring selections from the scores to the first five Star Trek films. As a preteen, the musicians I first memorized were not members of New Kids on the Block or the guys in Blur (that would come later) but instead the composers who worked on the Star Trek films. Jerry Goldsmith, James Horner, and Leonard Rosenman were actually the only three composers on this particular compilation, since the composer Cliff Eidelman was too new. He'd just done the music for the sixth Star Trek film, and I was going to have to buy that one as a separate tape when I saved up enough money, which, almost six months later, I did. In contrast to the previous, sunnier Star Trek movie scores, Eidelman's score for

The Undiscovered Country is super-dark, so much so I actually believed wholeheartedly it must have been the same guy who did the music for the 1989 *Batman* film. I was wrong about this, of course, since that score was composed by Danny Elfman, who has gone on to do lots of movies you probably like, while Eidelman's resume mostly consists of that one Star Trek movie and *Free Willy 3: The Rescue.**

If sci-fi television can prevent a child from enjoying kitchen-sink dramas, and sci-fi novels can make it hard for that same kid to start really digging literary realism, then imagine the amount of cultural malnourishment a kid can get from having *Star Trek: The Astral Symphony* as his first album. Once I had that tape in my Walkman, I never, ever, ever had to leave a certain kind of adventure. The only thing better than watching Star Trek was listening to it.

Like any greatest-hits album, *Star Trek: The Astral Symphony* wasn't actually for the true fan. As a grown-up, I'm a Beatles nut and absolutely detest the idea of the "Red" and "Blue" greatest-hits albums, since they mess up the risky progression of the Beatles' albums by only giving you the safe, popular stuff. Similarly, barely a year into playing my Star Trek album to the point of actually harming the tape itself, it dawned on me that it was a weird sampling of what this kind of music was actually all about, and I started doing some reading and buying more cassette tapes. The opening fanfare from *Star Trek V*, called "Life Is

---

* I've never seen this movie, but I guess Willy gets de-rescued somewhere in between *Free Willy* 1 and 2. I also love the fact that a guy who did the music for a great Star Trek film later had to work with preexisting music composed by Michael Jackson.

a Dream," I learned, was actually the same opening theme Jerry Goldsmith composed for *Star Trek: The Motion Picture.* This duh-dunt-dah-dunt-dah theme was later reworked as the opening for *Star Trek: The Next Generation,* and other than maybe the Alexander Courage ah-awww-ah-ah-ah-at-aww theme from the classic TV series, this is still the piece of music most associated with all of Star Trek. I'd also argue that *other* than the main theme to *Star Wars,* Jerry Goldsmith's "Life Is a Dream" is the *second* most recognizable sci-fi/fantasy theme song of all time.*

Sometime after 1992, I scored another greatest-hits album—this one all John Williams—containing selections not only from *Star Wars* but also from *Close Encounters of the Third Kind* and, excellently, *E.T.* In talking about big sci-fi fantasy scores, it's impossible to not try and figure out the whole John Williams dominance. As an adult, I worry there's an easy and often-trod cynical and acerbic route on this: John Williams music is used by Lucas and Spielberg *instead* of real writing and character development, and when you take it away, some of the more famous movie moments he's scored start to fall flat. As a sci-fi blogger I've seen this a million times: somebody posts a video of the last scene of *E.T.* or the last scene of *Star Wars* without the John Williams music and it's always presented like this big "gotcha" moment when you realize the music was just manipulating you into liking something that was stupid. But as a little kid, it's simply not true. The music isn't instead of the plot, or some kind of cheap trick. No. It's more like an

---

* Jerry Goldsmith also wrote the theme song for the fourth Star Trek TV show, *Star Trek: Voyager,* and it's my secret favorite Star Trek song.

ingredient, a spice, that certainly works on its own. There are elements of Star Wars that would be silly if isolated without the context, like watching Mark Hamill get hit with random pieces of Styrofoam by stagehands. But the score isn't like that; it might be part of the postproduction process, but it's also able to exist in its own dimension, removed from the visual narrative.

The Star Wars music sort of speaks for itself, but the most stirring of the John Williams themes for little me was *E.T.* I've got a massive soft spot for this particular movie, since my parents took me to see it at a drive-in when I was all of one year old and still in a car seat. I'm not saying I actually remember that particular screening, but I don't think it's a coincidence that I've devoted much of my professional career to science fiction stuff after the first movie I ever really "saw" was about a little kid hanging out with a friendly space alien. My mother also frequently claims that she wanted to name me Elliott after the character in the film, which is obviously one of those sweet mom lies that make no sense, since the movie obviously came out after I was born. Still, if you see a thirtysomething dude cruising around Brooklyn in a red Elliott hoodie humming to himself, there is a real chance it's me.*

What makes the *E.T.* music so great for a little kid is this naw-naa-nana-nanu-na-nooow sweeping, stringy fanfare that plays when the kids are riding on their bicycles and E.T. conjures up his handy bike-flying spell. My strongest, best childhood memories of listening to symphonic scores either while doing something shitty like mowing the lawn or, heroically, while

* There's also a chance it's like five million other girls and guys who live in Brooklyn (or Portland) and who own that same hoodie for the exact same reason.

riding a bicycle. When this song hit, I always, always, without fail imagined my bicycle flying. I could have been Elliott, but *E.T.* includes all the other kids, too. My other tapes, *Star Trek: The Astral Symphony* or *Great Sci-Fi TV Hits: Featuring Buck Rogers*, may have allowed me to picture my bike as shuttlecraft, or Earth Defense starfighter, but with the *E.T.* theme, the bicycle was just the bicycle. Williams's *E.T.* score is by no means his best, and I'd even go so far as to say it's his most generic, which is also why it's great. If you remember the themes from less-than-stellar '80s sci-fi movies, like *The Last Starfighter* (composed by Craig Safan) or *Masters of the Universe* (composed by Bill Conti), you'll notice they almost go out of their way to sound exactly like *E.T.* Plus, Williams seems to have almost ripped off himself when he did the score for the first Harry Potter film. Yes, "Hedwig's Theme" and "Harry's Wondrous World" are a little more haunting than *E.T.*'s cues "Chase/Escape," but if I'd never actually seen Harry Potter and only heard the score, I'd assume it was another movie about Elliott.*

◆

Kurt Vonnegut's fictional science fiction writer Kilgore Trout has a lot of funny and tragic traits, but the most telling of them

---

* There's also something about "Anakin's Theme," from the Star Wars prequels, that reminds me of Elliott, too, but maybe that's just because the *E.T.* aliens are randomly in that big Senate scene in *The Phantom Menace*, which technically makes *E.T.* and Star Wars exist in the same fictional universe. I know people have complained about this before, but what the fuck, everybody! If E.T. can live in Star Wars, then what's to stop the reverse from happening: a Star Wars movie rolling up on contemporary Earth?

all is in *Breakfast of Champions* when Vonnegut mentions, "Like most science-fiction writers, Kilgore Trout knew nothing about science." While this is super-insulting to a lot of persons both living and dead, I think it explains the relationship a genre film-score enthusiast has with classical music: we don't know anything about classical music, like at all. I thought I was totally alone on this fact until years later, with several sci-fi fantasy albums under my belt, I met someone who knew more about these movie scores than I did. And it was all because I'd decided to write a play.

I was sort of in college, and sort of involved in some theatre shenanigans at Arizona State University. Now, there's no reason to believe I would have actually been involved with this stuff if it hadn't been for my best friend, a guy who was, and is, a real playwright by the name of George. He had dared me to come up with an idea for a play to write with him, and knowing how much I talked about science fiction all the time, he prompted me to write a play that would be "like a sci-fi porno." I said okay, but he added a stipulation: "The constant sex has to come from a legitimate science fiction reason. You have to earn it." I was about twenty years old and accepted the challenge on the spot. I told him I'd have a treatment for an idea that would feature a "realistic reason for constant fucking in a science fiction narrative" by the morning. Obviously, my first thought was to cleverly disguise the plot of *Barbarella*, but I quickly realized that other than the effect Barbarella's promiscuousness had had on me (and the culture at large), it wasn't exactly rationalized all that well in the plot itself. Instead, I came up with Buck Falcon, better known to his friends as the interdimensional playboy Time Fucker.

George loved the idea and we wrote the "script" for the ten-minute play—*The Time Fucker Chronicles*—a few days later, probably while drinking a lot of Boone's Farm or box wine, or whatever you drink when you're really young and extremely proud of yourself for no reason. The "brilliant" science fiction conceit I'd give as to why Time Fucker needed to fuck so much—and across multiple time periods—was because he learns from a soothsayer that his family tree is actually the result of lots of time travel and sleeping around, but that if he doesn't end up becoming his own ancestor, he'll cease to exist. The soothsayer who tells him this is brutally murdered (naturally) right before he can tell Time Fucker the exact time period he needs to travel to in order to fulfill the paradox. So, like a horny Sam from *Quantum Leap*, Time Fucker has to travel through time and sleep with *anybody*. The play is both wonderful and wonderfully terrible and even though I later realized I'd unconsciously stolen most of the Time Fucker plot structure from a Robert A. Heinlein story, "All You Zombies—," I still occasionally worry that it might be the most original idea I've ever had.

When it came time to put the thing on, I took myself off the list of potential cast members, citing the fact that I'm a bad actor, and also would be completely wrong for Time Fucker.*

---

* I did have to end up with two lines or so as Time Fucker's boss, a character with an eyepatch named "Conrad," whom I'm pretty sure I lifted directly from the old Birdman cartoons.

George had already cast himself as the soothsayer and was insistent that we should cast someone tall, lanky, and uncool looking as Time Fucker. Looking back, this was totally genius, because if we'd actually recruited some thick-necked jock to play Time Fucker, the whole thing would have come across as creepy. And so, we were suddenly face-to-face with a guy named Dave, about six foot one, 135 pounds, with a concave chest and curly hair that sort of looked fake. His control of his body to walk like a complete idiot was astounding, and he even said he'd design his own costume for Time Fucker, which I was fine with as long as it was all silver.

Dave also had other opinions, and those opinions were connected with *what kind of music* would have come on at the beginning of the play. We were debuting *Time Fucker* at a tiny community theatre night, which was really just a glorified open mic night on campus. We were definitely going to freak everyone out with an off-book ten-minute play, complete with homemade costumes and a bunch of actors who weren't really even enrolled at the college. Most of the other acts that night were just going to be people holding scripts while sitting down and staring at the ground. *Time Fucker*, Dave and George decided, was going to make a splash, and that meant we needed some funny opening theme music. And here I discovered I had a kindred spirit in Dave. He was *obsessed* with movie scores. If you named a superhero movie that no one liked—*Supergirl*,* for example—he could name the composer in an instant. I was

* *Supergirl*, as opposed to *Barbarella,* is a movie that people think sucks, and they're totally right.

shocked to learn from Dave that *Jerry Goldsmith* had composed *Supergirl*. Dave was very familiar with the work of all my other Star Trek composers, too, and is the person who educated me on all the other wonderful scores Danny Elfman had done after Tim Burton's *Batman*. This doesn't mean he'd *seen* any of these movies, and that made Dave this bizarre evil mirror for me. He was playing the titular hero in my play, a man called Time Fucker, and he was interested in the same things I was, but for totally different reasons. Dave's involvement in *Time Fucker*, and specifically in choosing the musical cues, became bizarrely layered. And if you've ever read *Steppenwolf* by Hermann Hesse or seen a David Lynch movie, then you know how this goes: at any second you expect to wake up in another person's body, having thought your whole life was actually a dream, and really, you've been this other person your whole life. I'd like to say that I didn't see Dave as a darker, more specifically odd version of myself, but that's exactly what it was like. We both agreed that French horns made any soundtrack classier, and that there was almost no way a score could use a sax correctly. We both liked Howard Shore, but felt a little guilty about it. There was shame involved in these conversations, but on different levels.

And yet, all of Dave's suggestions for the opening music for *Time Fucker* felt wrong, and it was all down to the fact that he had no idea what the music actually connoted. Neither of us knew jack shit about real classical music, but Dave was suggesting things according to how they actually *sounded*. In every single way, this man was and is a greater lover of music— specifically this kind of music—than I was or ever could be.

But liking the theme song to your favorite TV show or movie is something I don't think most people thought about outside of the context of actually having seen a given show. Not all sci-fi scores were like John Williams's, where they could stand on their own and tell a story. Some could only be appreciated if you also knew there were ugly beige space suits associated with those notes or, in the case of *Supergirl*, black goo that actually infects its upbeat music.

Occasionally, I meet people who disprove this rule, like Dave, who actually just loves this style of music, but for the most part, dorky fans connect to and love music for the thing they're interested in because they're interested in the thing itself. This isn't to say theme music is inherently empty or meaningless or without skill. One of the most famous pieces of music—"Chariots of Fire"—was composed by Vangelis for the historical drama of the same name. I can hum this tune right now, and you probably can, too, but do you know what film Vangelis scored after *Chariots of Fire*? That's right: it was *Blade Runner*, the 1982 classic sci-fi movie directed by Ridley "Alien" Scott and starring Harrison Ford. I love the soundtrack to *Blade Runner*, and I think its ethereal oddity is part of what makes it so great, in the same way John Williams's music makes *Star Wars* or *Jurassic Park* work so well. Vangelis is obviously not a joke, and neither is John Williams, and, further, neither is Murray Gold, who currently scores *Doctor Who*, or Bear McCreary, who gave us those great drums (and a Jimi Hendrix cover) on the contemporary *Battlestar Galactica*. There is an inherent art to this kind of thing, and as is evidenced in my friend Dave's love of nearly every single score *ever*, it can be appreciated on its own.

Still, when it came to picking the opening music for *Time Fucker*, I was glad I knew my way around all these old sci-fi theme songs. Because when I selected Barry Gray's theme for *Space: 1999* as our opening *Time Fucker* fanfare, I knew everyone was going to love it. An often forgotten '70s show, *Space: 1999* is all about what happens to the people living on the moon when the moon gets blown out of orbit and starts flying around through space all on its own. How would you create theme music for a show that had as much outer space stuff as it had bell-bottoms? Easy: you start it off like a regular brass-heavy sci-fi fanfare, and then you kick in a funky porno-beat. I was the only one associated with the production of *Time Fucker* who knew the names of all the characters on *Space: 1999*, but at least Time Fucker himself knew the name of the composer.

✦

When I listen to *E.T.* I still want to fly, while most Star Trek music I'll put on just makes me feel safe with old childhood stuff. But if I ever happen to listen to the theme to *Space: 1999*, I weirdly now do *only* think of my own terribly embarrassing college play, and the time I discovered a bizarro version of myself living in my own hometown.

Baker Streets on Infinite Earths: Sherlock Holmes as the Eternal Sci-Fi Superhero

People born in the '80s who claim to have been into "cool" music as children are full of it. Those of us who were eight in 1989 might try to affect that we listened to the good stuff of the '80s (like the Smiths), but the fact is, we all just jammed real hard to Paula Abdul, New Kids on the Block, or the theme songs to TV shows we liked. And when it comes to my knowledge of Victorian literature—specifically Sherlock Holmes—I didn't "grow up" reading Sir Arthur Conan Doyle either, and if I've ever said that I did, I was lying. I read the entire canon of Holmes numerous times in my early twenties, but I got into Sherlock Holmes through popular science fiction, specifically the cartoon *The Real Ghostbusters.**

---

* This is exactly like learning about the Beatles by listening to Oasis.

In 1989, I must have been still reeling from dinosaur sex acts when I saw the episode of *The Real Ghostbusters* titled "Elementary, My Dear Winston," in which this show continued its endless obsession with confusing children about the meanings of certain English words, specifically the word "ghost" and, more aggressively, the word "real."* Rather than assert Sherlock Holmes was a real person, and have his ghost haunt a present-day cartoon New York, the show decided that the ghosts of Sherlock Holmes and Watson actually sprung into existence because enough people in the world believed in them. This means a fictional character could have a ghost, the same way fairies exist in *Peter Pan*, through the popularity of hysterical applause. This turned out to be handy for the Ghostbusters, because when the ghost of the evil Professor Moriarty showed up, it gave them something to do.

Hardly the best example of a science fiction tribute to the great detective Sherlock Holmes, this was still my first exposure to him, and from that moment, I totally placed Holmes

---

* The cartoon *The Real Ghostbusters*, which aired between 1986 and 1991, has its bizarre "real" prefix title for two reasons. First, there was a totally unrelated Filmation cartoon called *The Ghost Busters* (airing in various forms in 1975 and 1986) that needed to be retroactively made "fake" by asserting the one spun off from the film to be the real thing. More bizarrely, though, *The Real Ghostbusters* cartoon actually constructs a metafictional reality around the 1984 *Ghostbusters* film with the episode "Take Two," where it's revealed that the movie starring Bill Murray and company is actually just a film "based" on these "real" Ghostbusters in the cartoon. Coincidentally or not, this "reality gap" between two kinds of fiction is very similar to the fact that Watson publishes stories about Sherlock Holmes in the "reality" of the Sherlock Holmes stories. Now that I think about all of this, every single Sherlock Holmes pastiche can now be called "The Real Sherlock Holmes."

among the pantheon of other sci-fi heroes, right next to Batman and Mr. Spock. And, when I grew up, I discovered that I wasn't wrong. Just like the people in that random episode of *The Real Ghostbusters*, the enduring belief in Sherlock Holmes is just one piece of the mystery surrounding his undeniable connection to and inspiration for science fiction.

Science fiction relationships to Sherlock Holmes might be contemporarily obvious to anyone who is familiar with the Internet's fixation on moving GIFs of Benedict Cumberbatch's cheekbones. The brilliant BBC adaptation of the famous detective—*Sherlock*—is cowritten by Steven Moffat, who (as of this writing) is also the showrunner for that quirky, long-running little-British-science-fiction-show-that-could, *Doctor Who*. I used to love this fact so much that I had a giant photograph of Cumberbatch and Matt Smith from *Doctor Who* hugging Steven Moffat as my screen wallpaper on my computer for like six months in 2011. Fans of both shows have been salivating for a science fiction crossover between the Time Lord from the planet Gallifrey and Cumberbatch's Sherlock since 2010, but connections to *Doctor Who*'s titular hero and Holmes go back to *Doctor Who*'s inception in 1963. The Doctor is a renegade Time Lord, while Sherlock Holmes is an amateur consulting detective. Both are heroes who reject the rules of the fields they work in—Holmes works in crime, the Doctor in space-time—and neither has a great deal of respect for social niceties. Plus, unlike Britain's other pseudo-literary hero, James Bond, neither the Doctor nor Sherlock Holmes is all that interested in getting laid. In the pantheon of superheroes in general,

Sherlock Holmes might not be unique in his asexual, low-violence behavior, but he was one of the first, if not *the* first, archetypes for a geeky, brainy person winning the day in one pop adventure after another. Still, just because Sherlock is brainy and asexual, it doesn't suddenly grant him the ability to travel in time and space.

The literary, original, brilliant Sherlock found in the pages of Conan Doyle's fifty-six short stories and four novels is initially presented as an ignoramus when it comes to the one thing you'd probably associate with science fiction: outer space! The "real" Sherlock Holmes doesn't know jack shit about the astronomical workings of the planets and stars, and in the first Holmes appearance ever (the novel *A Study in Scarlet*), he accosts Watson on the subject: "What the deuce is it to me? You say that we go round the sun. If we went round the moon it would not make a pennyworth of difference to me or to my work." Holmes likens his mind to an attic, one he can only fill with the right kinds of "furniture" necessary for his occupation. Cumberbatch's incarnation of the detective updated this image for the twenty-first century by saying, "This is my hard drive," indicating that his "mind palace" has information limitations. But even if Holmes does get an F in astronomy, his connections to science fiction aren't casual. When you break it down, Holmes's sci-fi message is in his methods.

From the years 1887 to 1927, Holmes dies and comes back; faces a variety of criminals, schemes, and ghoulish mysteries; and also becomes a nuisance to Inspector Lestrade and the rest of Scotland Yard. But perhaps his most relevant contribution to science fiction is the invention of something Holmes calls "the science of deduction."

Holmes believes any mystery can be approached, and a solution deduced, scientifically, by gathering necessary data and drawing conclusions based on logic and reason. In the Doyle stories, the science of deduction usually works and serves as the basic premise for nearly every single Holmes adventure. Instead of creating a detective who arrives at the answers through intuition or moxie, Doyle asserted a different premise with the Holmes stories—what if the detective discovers the answers scientifically? What kind of adventures might he have? Looked at from this semantic angle, the original canon of Sherlock Holmes is already science fiction, as science is being used *fictionally*.

Lyndsay Faye—Holmes expert, author of the Holmes pastiche *Dust and Shadow*, and member of numerous Sherlock Holmes organizations (notably the Baker Street Irregulars and the Adventuresses of Sherlock Holmes)—explains: "Sherlock Holmes and science fiction have always been tied together because Doyle was writing about the cutting edge of forensic science . . . For example, Holmes is in the very act of perfecting the world's first infallible blood test when Watson meets him."

Still, the hard science of old-school Sherlock Holmes doesn't always stack up against the forensic labs of today, as much as Cumberbatch's or Jonny Lee Miller's twenty-first-century Sherlocks might attempt to bring it all up to speed. And that's because there are occasionally problems in the methodology.

According to Zachary Pirtle, program analyst at NASA, "Real science still doesn't work in the strictly deductive way that Holmes describes; for the best scientific questions, there are no straightforward answers, and a lot of the hard work comes from simply trying to imagine new possibilities." And yet Holmes is constantly affirming his belief in the improbable, indicating his imagination is among his intellectual tools. In "The Adventure of the Bruce-Partington Plans," Holmes—lacking any evidence—conceives the fantastic notion of a body being placed on the roof of a moving train. In the Granada Television adaptation of the same story, after the hypothesis is proven true, Holmes (as portrayed by the late Jeremy Brett) grins broadly and shouts, "Imagination, Watson! Imagination!" So, while Sherlock Holmes is a walking computer full of logic and reason, he also values imagination in the same way a sci-fi writer might. Five-time Hugo Award winner Mike Resnick asserts that Sherlock Holmes appeals to fans and specifically writers of science fiction because Holmes "is cerebral rather than physical. And he has overcome what seems a tendency to be a social maladroit, which latter defines a lot of writers, many of whom chose their profession for that very reason."

At this point, we have to talk about Star Trek, and specifically Mr. Spock. Spock's lack of emotions and his ability to get to the bottom of various outer space mysteries certainly make him the Sherlock Holmes of the future, but it wasn't until the '60s were over and the Star Trek films got going that the Holmesian connections to Spock became totally clear. Everybody knows the best Star Trek film is 1982's *The Wrath of Khan*, which was written and directed by Nicholas Meyer.* But you might not know that Nicholas Meyer is also the author of three excellent Sherlock Holmes pastiches: *The Seven-Per-Cent Solution*, *The Canary Trainer*, and *The West End Horror*. A few years ago, I chatted with Meyer extensively about Sherlock Holmes and he said this: "Because the Holmes stories deal with chemistry and scientific stuff, it's a hop-skip-and-a-jump over to actual science fiction." And he would know, because he put actual Sherlock Holmes dialogue into Mr. Spock's mouth in his other Star Trek movie, *Star Trek VI: The Undiscovered Country*. When faced with an intergalactic whodunit, Spock quotes Holmes by saying, "An ancestor of mine maintained that when you eliminate the impossible, whatever remains, however improbable, must be the truth." Meyer claims that "the link between Spock and Holmes was obvious to everyone. I just sort of made it official." But it's more than just a link. In his 1991 Star Trek movie, Nicholas Meyer casually has Spock imply that Sherlock Holmes is *literally* his ancestor, which actually works just fine, since, according to Star Trek lore, Spock is half human on his mother's side, meaning Sherlock Holmes could actually be his great-great-great-great-great-grandfather. And when I needled Meyer to tell me who Spock's great-great-great-great-great-grandmother was, he said that it was "of course, Irene Adler."†

---

* Famously, Nick Meyer received no screenwriting credit for *Star Trek II: The Wrath of Khan*, and that's because he offered to rewrite the messed-up screenplay from scratch in an amount of time that made it impossible to negotiate union rights. Meyer didn't care about getting the credit; he just wanted a script he could direct. Make no mistake, this excellent movie is his baby, 100 percent.

† Irene Alder is a blackmailer in the Doyle story "A Scandal in Bohemia." She's frequently the love interest in Holmes adaptations. She was

What's fun about this notion is that it posits the original Star Trek in the same fictional universe as that of Sherlock Holmes, which is a kind of variation on what Sherlock Holmes fans have been doing for almost a century—playing the great "game," in which everyone pretends Sherlock Holmes is a real person, and that Sir Arthur Conan Doyle was just Dr. John Watson's literary agent. This game has been going on since the founding of the Baker Street Irregulars, the oldest Sherlock Holmes fan organization in the world and, in some ways, the original comic con. Since 1934 (and probably before) "game" is seldom mentioned outright, but simply meant to be the default way to explore Sherlockian scholarship.

Nicholas Meyer took this long-running practical joke so far that when he published his first Holmes pastiche, *The Seven-Per-Cent Solution*, in 1976, the dust jacket actually read "by John H. Watson, M.D., edited by Nicholas Meyer." In 2002, yours truly read this novel after picking it up at a used bookstore and was utterly baffled by the purported authorship. I'd always thought John Watson was a fictional character! What's this? He's real?

The Internet in 2002 wasn't as forthcoming with this information as it is today, and even if you read Leslie Klinger's excellently edited 2003 edition of *The Complete Annotated Sherlock Holmes*, the footnotes will be partially surreal if you

---

portrayed by Charlotte Rampling in 1976's *Sherlock Holmes in New York* and by Gayle Hunnicutt in 1984's "A Scandal in Bohemia." More recently, we've seen Rachel McAdams as Adler in both of the Sherlock films starring Robert Downey Jr. Lara Pulver played her on *Sherlock*, and Natalie Dormer on *Elementary*, where Irene Adler also has ANOTHER secret identity. Imagine whichever Irene Adler actress you like as Spock's maternal ancestor.

didn't happen to catch his brief note at the beginning where he winks to you and references "the gentle fiction" of the game, thus reminding you that all three volumes of these giant books will have "research" strewn throughout that is, in essence, built on a big old game of make-believe. Just as in that *Real Ghostbusters* episode, everybody loves pretending Sherlock Holmes is alive in some way, shape, or form. Even if he's living in Star Trek's future's past.

Sadly, if you take *Star Trek: The Next Generation* as being part of the same canon as the classic *Star Trek*, then Sherlock Holmes goes right back to being a fictional character. In two memorable episodes of *The Next Generation*, the android (robot) Mr. Data outright impersonates Sherlock Holmes, casually destroying the theory that Star Trek and Sherlock Holmes occupy the same universe and are governed by the same fictional god. This is a bit of a bummer, but if we can think of Star Trek's flirtations with trying to subsume Sherlock Holmes into its own canon as a thought experiment, an even more compelling and slightly frightening notion emerges: the world can't exist without Sherlock Holmes. Any conception of a reality without Sherlock Holmes has to be science fiction, specifically. And if that happens in TV, it's always, paradoxically, on shows featuring Sherlock Holmes.

Take *Sherlock*, starring Benedict Cumberbatch. Surely, this is a science fiction program, because it takes place in an *alternate dimension* in which Sherlock Holmes is not a famous literary character and no one in the twenty-first century has heard of him. Ditto for *Elementary*. What kind of planet Earth is this? Not the twenty-first century I live in. In fact, you could assume that the crime of these alternate twenty-first centuries is far more rampant than the crime in our dimension. Without the heroic inspiration of Sherlock Holmes in the late 1800s—either as fictional character or real person—any dimension on planet Earth is going to suffer from a bleaker future. Nicholas Meyer describes the original Holmes stories as a "secular religion," because through them "the world can be understood." And while I personally agree with him, it doesn't actually matter what Nicholas Meyer and I think, because the proof is in the zeitgeist itself. Even when you've got a hospital TV show like *House*, some sort of faux Sherlock Holmes saunters in. He's everywhere! Sherlock Holmes is, bizarrely, stuck in our cultural programming so hard that it makes you wonder if some kind of divine scientific creator didn't put him there. If Cumberbatch's Sherlock were to die, he'd immediately come back to life. Oh wait. That already happened. Even Conan Doyle tried to kill off Holmes in the original story "The Final Problem," and the universe just didn't allow for it.* It could be magic keeping Holmes alive, or it could be science fiction.

Over the years, science fiction authors have delighted in figuring out ways for Holmes to remain more literally immortal. In Susan Casper's "Holmes Ex Machina," the detective is reconstructed as a holographic computer program and assists in solving a minor mystery relating to missing film canisters. In "Moriarty by Modem" by Jack Nimersheim, another

---

* This is a little like Harry Potter. It is my belief that J. K. Rowling will be forced to write another Harry Potter novel by the universe or the same god that is keeping Holmes alive. You heard it here first. She'll do it before the decade is out.

complex computer program is created to emulate the thought patterns and theories of Sherlock Holmes, but sadly a parallel computer virus called "Moriarty" is also accidentally created and loosed upon a cute 1990s version of cyberspace that sort of sounds a little like Tron minus Jeff Bridges (and thus, minus the charm).

Further proof that some version of Sherlock Holmes and Watson is a weird linchpin holding the entire universe together shows up in Neil Gaiman's trippy story "A Study in Emerald." Like Meyer mashing up Holmes with Star Trek, Gaiman spins some Lovecraft by imagining a Victorian London ruled by the infamous many-tentacled Cthulhu. Here, there are numerous Cthulhu, and one of them, a prince, has been murdered. As in the plot of *A Study in Scarlet*, two men—who we THINK are Holmes and Watson—have just become flatmates, perfect strangers to each other who are rapidly thrust into their inaugural adventure. Gaiman toys with his characters' awareness of the existence of alternate realities: "I have a feeling we were meant to be together," one says, "that we have fought the good fight, side by side, in the past or future, I do not know." The twist here is that we figure out by the end that this isn't Holmes and Watson at all, but rather, fucking Moriarty and his right-hand man and trigger-finger, Colonel Sebastian Moran.

If there's a higher purpose to science fiction, other than to entertain, one aim is usually to understand the human experience through hyperbolic stories. Science fiction has always been highly equipped to handle far-out problems by viewing culture and individuals through the lens of technology or fantastical concepts. Explaining life as we know it, or might one day live it, is certainly the task of all good science fiction. Similarly, the stories and enduring character of Sherlock Holmes provide a lens through which the human experience can be occasionally deduced or explained. In an unreasonable world, the greatest science fiction can frequently comfort us, while at the same time forcing us to confront our greatest fears. And the ultimate impact of Sherlock Holmes is the same: even when he doesn't exist, the ghost of Sherlock Holmes is still stubbornly, and improbably, real.

All You McFlys: A *Back to the Future* Theory of Everything

I'm living in 2015 and everyone I know is complaining that they don't have their own hoverboard yet. Because 2015 is the year Marty and Doc travel to in *Back to the Future Part II*, it has permanently become a version of the future everyone loves to fetishize. There are flying cars, flying skateboards, and guys wearing two ties instead of one. Yet *Back to the Future*'s "future" was originally "the present." Not only did *Back to the Future* create a permanent future with 2015, it also created a permanent past (the 1950s) and present (1980s). This is partly because the entire *Back to the Future* trilogy encompasses every single genre imaginable.

Think about it. It's an adventure. It's a mystery. It's a comedy. It's a romance. It's a romantic comedy. It's *obviously* science fiction. Somehow it's a fucking western. This isn't to say the whole *Back to the Future* thing is perfect or even objectively "good." It's just that if we needed to shoot something into space that represented what American pop culture was interested in from the late twentieth century until now, all three *Back to the Future* films would explain us—positively and negatively—better than pretty much anything else. I don't have the chalkboard Doc uses in the second movie, so instead, I'll attempt to break down everything you need to know about *Back to the Future* into easy (hard) to understand sections. So, we need first to understand why we love it so much in order to understand what we still don't understand about it.

Let's Talk About Fake Nostalgia

In the first movie, Marty McFly creates a better future for his family by subtly altering their past. In the second film, Marty attempts to rescue his own negative future, while repairing an alternate present. Finally, part three sees Marty and his time-traveling friend Doc simultaneously embrace and mock the values of the most cliché part of America's past: the Old West. As much as Marty and Doc rip apart the meaning of cause and effect throughout all their time traveling, their values don't actually change one iota throughout the films, and despite all the conflicts they endure, both exert maximum control over their lives. The obvious irony here is that for a series of films supposedly about pivotal moments of choice in life, the stories aren't really contemplative about these choices because the main characters experience only temporary consequences. In *Back to the Future*, if your life didn't turn out the way you wanted, that can be fixed.

Like the audience, Marty retains the memories of each of

his various contradictory timelines, meaning he can constantly pat himself on the back for how great he is at avoiding catastrophe. The reason why we adore Marty McFly and Doc isn't just because Michael J. Fox and Christopher Lloyd are crazy charming in these movies (they obviously are), but because their adventures combine the two things Americans love: getting our way and fake nostalgia.

In the final scene of *Back to the Future Part III*, Doc Brown—leaning over his sweet-ass steampunk hover train—enthusiastically tells Jennifer: "Your future hasn't been written yet! No one's has! Your future is whatever you make it!"

It's all pretty inspirational and I cried quite a lot as a child when Doc said that stuff.* However, if Doc was being honest about his "real" life, and not winking at the camera for our benefit, he might have said this: "Also, your *past* isn't written either, Jennifer. Marty and I changed the past like six different times!"

Like so many important geeky phenomena, it's hard to talk about the cultural importance of *Back to the Future* without getting into the nerdy specifics of its plot holes. But unlike something like Star Wars, where certain problems can be explained with in-universe analysis, *Back to the Future* can only be discussed with ourselves (the audience) firmly in the conversation, and that's because everything about these movies is so obviously unrealistic. Am I saying I find the galaxy-spanning illiterate culture of Star Wars, a place where full-on magic is

---

* Who am I kidding. I cry as an adult, too. I also cried when I saw Christopher Lloyd speak at New York Comic Con in 2012.

commonplace, a more *realistic* world than *Back to the Future*? Yes, and understanding this is the first step to understanding the Ouroboros of this film series.

Hill Valley as the American every-city is an easy place to start. It's located in California, but exactly where isn't clear. We never see the ocean, nor does it seem like anybody ever talks about cities outside of Hill Valley. In the alternate "present," in *Back to the Future Part II*, Biff makes a mention of "Switzerland," suggesting a world outside of Hill Valley, which is an uncommon move for the series. You might wonder why Biff decided to build his big empire in Hill Valley and not move to Vegas, but that would ignore a bigger question as to why so many generations of these characters' families stay in the same town. Like Biff, Marty McFly is similarly Hill Valley–centric, because even though he possesses all the other realistic qualities of a teenager,* Marty has no desire to get out of this small town and head somewhere else. In fact, Marty McFly's "big dreams" in the first film are simply to have a fancy pickup truck and to maybe someday live in a housing community like Hilldale with Jennifer. (Here, Marty is the anti–Luke Skywalker.)

Marty McFly and his girlfriend, Jennifer Parker, have endlessly suburban values, with aspirations that are humble and 100 percent relatable to most people. This is why everyone loves these movies: nothing happens outside of Hill Valley, because the American experience (in the mind of all Americans) is exactly the same way. If you grew up in the suburbs of America, you know there are people who don't think of

---

* Other than drinking. Marty never really drinks.

anything outside of their town. It's really easy to imagine George Saunders or Steven Millhauser writing about Marty and Jennifer.

The creation of *Back to the Future*'s fake nostalgia begins with the way Hill Valley looks: exactly like every town you've ever seen on American television. It feels familiar, because television and giant films make things really familiar, really quickly. So, when we journey into Hill Valley's past in the first movie, you feel *doubly* nostalgic, because even though you've just seen this fake town, you feel like you already know it, and now you're getting misty about seeing what it was like in 1955. There's also nothing jarring about the transition between the 1985 music and the 1955 music in *Back to the Future* because Huey Lewis and the News is also a band made of pure fake nostalgia.

We think of the 1980s as being represented by a lot of different types of music—the Clash, Blondie, Bowie, Michael Jackson—but Huey Lewis and the News specifically represents a music thing in the '80s: that of being soft and retro on purpose, and not in a way that is remotely cool. This isn't to say Huey Lewis and the News isn't "good," simply that I feel like Kenny Loggins could kick Huey's ass. Huey Lewis and the News is the safest of the safe '80s music, to put it another way, the American version of Coldplay in 1985.* These days, nostalgia for Huey Lewis and the News has only grown and that's because there's a near invisible line between pop art being "timeless" and benefiting from fake nostalgia. Because everyone alive today is obsessed with pop art that came out after World War II, the 1950s will

---

* I happen to love both Coldplay and Huey Lewis. Just to be clear.

always look good in films, and *Back to the Future* takes advantage of this by creating wacky anachronisms. For example, seeing Marty's purple Calvin Klein underwear shock Lorraine's 1955 sensibilities is a funny joke to audiences in 1985 and only gets funnier as this version of 1955 and its anachronisms both continue to recede farther and farther into the past. Not only does Marty have the Calvin Klein underwear, but he calls himself "Calvin Klein." In *Back to the Future Part III*, hanging out in 1885, Marty calls himself "Clint Eastwood," which is funny even if you've never seen *The Good, the Bad and the Ugly*. Add to this the fact that alternate-universe Biff is watching *The Good, the Bad and the Ugly* on TV in *Back to the Future Part II*, proving that both the reference and the reference-heavy joke ("Clint Eastwood") are self-contained in these movies. Which is one way to build a fake nostalgia machine: layer your cultural references inside of your anachronistic jokes.

In the context of thinking of this as a science fiction movie, you could say that it's not that super weird that everything takes place in Hill Valley. Even Doc mentions that there seems to be some universal significance to the date November 12, 1955, the day when the clock tower is struck by lightning, Marty and Doc first "meet," and Marty's parents go to the Enchantment Under the Sea Dance. This *temporal* location becomes the destination (and occasionally the origin) for the entire *Back to the Future* universe. So, it follows that the physical location of Hill Valley itself is also super important, the journey to Mecca that is also itself Mecca. This works from a literary angle if we think of *Back to the Future* as intentionally nonrealistic in its metaphoric tone. There's not a world outside of Hill Valley *at all*, because just as in Neil Gaiman's *Coraline*, you can walk away from "the other house," but the farther you get away, the sooner you'll find yourself walking back toward it. If José Saramago had decided to write a novel about paradoxes, he would have probably manufactured a place similar to Hill Valley.

Reoccurring tendencies throughout the history of Hill Valley also help to construct the fake nostalgia of these films while cementing the surrealist nature of everyone's biographies. Doc and Marty's friendship is the most echoing, and not just because they're time travelers. Essentially their relationship is more like father and son than best buddies, which means there are effectively two nerdy dads, Doc and George McFly. Even though Marty clearly prefers his fake dad (Doc) to his real dad (George). Still, fake dad or not, Marty and Doc are already hanging out in the original *Back to the Future*, and it's never clear from Marty's perspective how they first met. Without thinking about it too hard, you could just say that various time-travel paradoxes have "always" happened, meaning they were always friends even if they don't know when and where they first met. Here, we've arrived at the best part of any discussion about time-travel stories: what's the deal with the paradoxes and just how many of them are we juggling in these movies?

Let's Talk About Paradoxes

Why Marty and Doc are even friends at all represents something of an ontological or "bootstraps" paradox, where cause and effect become utterly unclear. We don't know if

Marty and Doc "met" in 1955 or sometime in the 1980s prior to the start of the first film. Because we see Marty meet Doc in 1955, we're forced to infer that some kind of information paradox is at work. But since we aren't given enough information about what Marty *believed* their relationship was before going back in time in 1985, we're not sure. This isn't a mistake or anything, at all, because again, the fact that Doc and Marty were "already" friends at the start of the first movie means that cause and effect are being subverted before the actual time travel is even fucking introduced, which is totally brilliant. Listen, *Back to the Future* created fake nostalgia and a paradox just by having you believe this teenager and this mad scientist were already friends FOR NO GOOD REASON AT ALL. At the very start, Doc is good old Doc, somebody with whom Marty has always hung out and who we love and trust implicitly.

Now, consider the simple fact that a contemporary blockbuster movie made in America would never ever attempt this now. These days, big genre films always start with a very detailed origin story of the hero, and the relationships with all the heroes' friends are firmly established before the movie wraps up its generic plot. In fact, that is the entire plot to J. J. Abrams's *Star Trek* in 2009: let's get to know everybody! *Back to the Future* is so slick that it gets away with us believing these character relationships exist right away, even though the relationships seem totally unrealistic. The relationship between Kirk and Spock in the Abrams *Star Trek* is way more realistic than the relationship between Marty and Doc, but we like Marty and Doc *more* because their relationship works off of fake nostalgia, whereas Kirk and Spock in the Abrams *Star Trek* are actually fueled by the real nostalgia for old *Star Trek*.* This isn't to say that a possible remake of *Back to the Future* would be successful, but its character dynamics might be presented in a way that is more realistic. Most important: I've seen Christopher Lloyd field the question as to who should play Doc in a *Back to the Future* remake and he always says "me." I'd say that means he's probably a real time traveler.

The Biff Tannen Family Tree Paradox

Throughout the trilogy, the Tannen family terrorizes the McFly family in five separate time periods: 1885, 1955, 1985, 2015, and an alternate version of 1985 in which Biff Tannen rules Hill Valley from his hot tub. But who the fuck are Biff's parents? And where did all the Tannens come from anyway? In the original *Back to the Future*, Thomas F. Wilson brilliantly plays a fortysomething Biff Tannen in 1985, and a teenage Biff in 1955, both providing nice McFly nemesis parallels. In 1985, Biff is George McFly's biggest problem, but in 1955, Biff becomes Marty's problem, and thanks to time travel Biff and Marty are "the same age." Similarly, when Marty travels forward in time to 2015 in *Back to the Future Part II*, he's confronted with Griff Tannen, a teenager about Marty's age who is Biff's grandson. In a flip from the first film—where Marty's

---

* Which is also fake, in a way, since a lot of people who liked *Star Trek* 2009 still don't care about 1960s *Star Trek*.

father George is Biff's age—Marty's son, Marty Jr.,* is exactly Griff's age. Oddly, there is no member of the Tannen family who is *Marty's* age. Or, at least not one we see. In 1985—the temporal location where all this "starts"—Biff appears to be unmarried, and yet in 2015, it's confirmed that Griff in 2015 is the grandchild of Biff, thanks to Old Biff's quip "Whatdya think, Griff calls me gramps for his health?"

Yet, we have no idea who Griff's parents are. Presumably, one of Griff's parents should be Marty's age in 1985 and hanging around with people Marty knows in high school. Could there be a member of the Tannen family in Marty's band, the Pinheads? Could Jennifer Parker actually be friends with Biff's *daughter*? Early script ideas for *Back to the Future Part II* did include a "Tiff Tannen," who would probably have existed in 1985 and served as the Tannen foil for Marty's generation, but as it stands, we never got to see her.

Weirder still is the fact that in *Back to the Future Part II* we see that 1955 teenage Biff lives with his grandmother, and like his descendant, Griff, has no parents to speak of. Griff's immediate progenitor maybe just didn't get screentime, so therefore might still exist. But dialogue from *Back to the Future Part II* tells us the house where Biff lives with his grandmother belongs to "the only Tannen in the [phone] book," leading us to believe the only Tannens who actually live in Hill Valley in 1955 are

---

* What if Crispin Glover had done *Back to the Future Part II* and played Marty Jr.? How much weirder of a movie would that have been? Tom Wilson got to play his own grandson, so why not? Next, imagine Crispin Glover with a crazy Irish accent playing Seamus McFly in *Back to the Future Part III*.

Biff and his grandmother, making Biff's origin, at that point in the story, even more unclear than Griff's. I suppose we have to assume Biff and Griff have parents, but that's no fun.

In *Back to the Future Part III*, we meet Buford "Mad Dog" Tannen (though we did hear him mentioned in an alternate version of 1985 in *BTTFII*) in the Old West of 1885. Mad Dog, we're told, is Biff's great-grandfather and this highlights another conspicuous missing branch in the Tannen family tree. If this is Biff's great-grandfather, that means he *might* be the father of Biff's grandmother in 1955. However, maybe not. Biff's grandmother—the only Tannen in the book, remember— may have married into that name. If we journey outside the canon of the films, this supposedly gets explained, since the *Back to the Future* video game "reveals" Biff's father was a mobster named "Kid" Tannen, who we're supposed to infer was Mad Dog's son. The only problem with this is that you're pretty sure that Mad Dog will be hanged after Marty and Doc split 1885 in *BTTFIII*, and even though we don't *know* if Mad Dog had a family, wife, or something, we certainly don't see them. Biff and Griff's only male ancestor probably dies in 1885 and from that point on, the Tannen family seems to only have a representative alive from every *other* generation, at any given time.

The conspicuous absence of various branches of Biff's family tree can mean only one thing: Biff is both his own "father" and his own "son." In *BTTFII* Old Biff from 2015 steals the DeLorean and travels to 1955 to give young Biff the sport's almanac that will make him all sorts of money in the "future." Now, just because we don't see Old Biff time traveling elsewhere doesn't mean that he doesn't. I know, I know. Conspiracy theories always tend to work better when there's less evidence, and this one is a great conspiracy theory. But I think the best solution to this is that Biff figures out that he's the product of a paradox and, as a result, has to ensure his own existence by becoming his own ancestor and descendant. This means the missing parts of Biff's family tree are just him, time traveling. Genetically, I've been told this is actually impossible, as you'll never create a perfect genetic replica of yourself. Still, that quintessential Robert A. Heinlein time-travel short story "All You Zombies—" features a character who is his own father and mother and also gives birth to him/herself. If you can't do these things in science fiction, I ask, what is the point of science fiction?

The George McFly Writing Career Pseudo-Paradox

We know George McFly is the density—err—*destiny* of Lorraine Banes, but his initial timeline did not have him becoming a celebrated science fiction author. When Marty visits the 1955 version of his father in the first *Back to the Future*, George has all the traditional traits of a total dork: bad haircut, lame clothes, no confidence, and, of course, an interest in science fiction. Famously, Marty uses science fiction to convince George he is an alien with a special message: Marty impersonates a faux alien with his low-budget version of a Star Trek/Star Wars mash-up. Without this one event, Marty would not have been able to put the timeline back on course, meaning science fiction inside of science fiction saves the day in *Back to the Future*. But, it gets better, because in the new timeline Marty has accidentally caused his father to become a science fiction writer and, judging by the state of the McFly household, a reasonably successful one, too!

Some naysayers may point out that *A Match Made in Space* is only George McFly's first novel, which wouldn't account for the comfortable living environment. It has been asserted that it shouldn't have taken him this long to get the novel done and published. However, it's possible that George McFly, after his encounter with Darth Vader from the planet Vulcan, went on to become a hot short-story writer like Harlan Ellison or Kurt Vonnegut. Hell, George McFly may have been selling scripts to *The Outer Limits* or *The Twilight Zone*, assuming such things exist in the *Back to the Future* world, which they probably do, because we saw an episode of *The Honeymooners* in the first movie. This era in George McFly's science fiction writing would certainly fit the post-1955 time frame, and the fact that the McFlys live in California, near the TV world action, makes it all the more plausible. You could even say that in Marty's reality, George McFly sued both George Lucas and Gene Roddenberry over the use of his original concepts "Darth Vader" (Star Wars) and the planet "Vulcan" (Star Trek). This would explain why George McFly has a ton of money *before* his first novel comes out. And if Marty McFly, through his father, actually created both Star Trek and Star Wars via paradox, *Back to the Future* becomes a work of fake nonfiction and übermetafiction simultaneously.

The Jennifer Parker Paradox

The actress who plays Jennifer Parker in *Back to the Future* is different from the actress who plays her in *Back to the Future Parts II and III.* In the first movie she's played by Claudia Wells, who's replaced by Elisabeth Shue in the sequels. Most fans would probably consider Elisabeth Shue to be the "real" Jennifer the same way people consider Maggie Gyllenhaal to be the "real" Rachel in the Batman movies and not Katie Holmes. The explanation for this is confusing: writer Bob Gale and director Robert Zemeckis supposedly couldn't get Claudia Wells back, but who really knows. The craziest thing about this Jennifer switcheroo is that you'd never notice it if you'd only seen these films once as a little kid. *Back to the Future* succeeds at creating the ultimate fake nostalgia by totally reshooting the ending sequence of the first film almost five years after the fact with a totally new actress. Still, Claudia Wells did the voice of Jennifer in 2010/2011's *Back to the Future: The Game*, in which she reclaims some of her canonical Jennifer status. This more than anything, I think, is proof that the alternate universe in these movies directly blends over into what we pretend to call the real world.

More troubling than the Jennifer switch, though, is the fact that the character of Jennifer herself is almost worse than tertiary to the plots of any of the films. In the original *BTTF*, she's nothing more than Marty's trophy girlfriend. In the second film, she's literally unconscious for most of the action, and she only appears at the very end of the third film. Marty is never unfaithful to Jennifer, but she is something of a sleeping Penelope throughout these movies, unwittingly waiting for Marty to come home from his Odyssey. This is obliviously and totally sexist in the worst way, but in a film series that plays with oedipal themes from the very beginning (Marty's mom wants to screw him), progressive roles for women are unsurprisingly scarce. Not all fake nostalgia is good, and in fact, when it comes to gender and race, *Back to the Future* represents our past pop tendencies all too accurately.

The Past and the Future: Not Quite Perfect

Marty McFly is a person who is clearly like thirty years old and pretending to be in high school. In fairness, all big movies set in "high school" have this problem; everyone in *Grease* looks like an actor pretending to be in a fake high school, which in *Grease* is sort of the point. But we already know that *Back to the Future* has a more surreal approach to all of this, and the most surreal thing about it is the almost total absence of black people.

To say that *Back to the Future* is a racist movie since it only has a few black characters isn't exactly fair. The white people in *Back to the Future* (nearly everyone) are almost as badly stereotyped as the few black characters. I think imaginary *Back to the Future* black characters got lucky dodging being in this bizarre representation of whiteness. Because it's here where

Back to the Future's fake nostalgia gets sad, but is totally accurate in terms of how pop culture often hews. Anyone who's read any history is aware that America in 1955 was worse for blacks than it was in 1985, but the 1955 Marty McFly travels to in the first and second movies is super-rosy. There are black guys in the 1955 backing band, and we're told that Goldie Wilson, a black guy sweeping the floors in the diner, will soon be the mayor of Hill Valley. We also learn one of the guys in the band is Chuck Berry's "cousin" Marvin Berry, and that the authorship of "Johnny B. Goode" is actually the result of a time-travel paradox. Obviously, in real life, Chuck Berry didn't write "Johnny B. Goode" thanks to some time-traveling white guy, but shit, it sounds pretty racist to think *Back to the Future* asserts that very fact. Marty and Doc and literally everyone else in this movie are allowed to just casually "exist" and even make their lives better through their wacky technology and funny adventures. Meanwhile, Marvin Berry and Goldie Wilson are required to "dream big," rather than actually live big. *Back to the Future* is accidentally trying to achieve paradoxical revisionism that makes white people feel better about the past. This is fake nostalgia for something the (white) target audience didn't experience—in the case of racial equity, because it didn't exist.

Back to the Future isn't a bad movie series at all, though, and if you can't tell, I totally love it. But, if there's one thing I feel is important about love, it is understanding the deeply flawed characteristics of things you love, so you can better understand yourself, and how best to enjoy yourself. There's a great episode of *Star Trek: Deep Space Nine* that helped me see this and think about how a progressive, forward-thinking person can make sense of the occasionally scary side of fake nostalgia. In Star Trek, they've got the holodeck: a souped-up virtual reality place where endless fantasies can happen. And in an episode of *Deep Space Nine* called "Badda-Bing, Badda-Bang," there's a holographic (fake) 1962 nightclub called Vic's that a bunch of the Star Trek people like hanging out in. The main character of *Deep Space Nine*—if you're unaware—is Star Trek's only black lead, Avery Brooks as Ben Sisko, the guy who runs the space station, plus a spaceship, both full-time, while also being a single dad.* In this episode he argues with his girlfriend, Kasidy Yates (Penny Johnson), about the morality of enjoying the fake 1962 nightclub, as such enjoyment essentially requires pretending racism didn't exist back then. Sisko takes the stance I think most of us would take now: historical entertainment that eschews or avoids the unpleasant racial truths of the past is bullshit. However, Yates gives Sisko a counterargument: enjoying this form of entertainment can be empowering, as long as no one forgets what the real truth was.

I think for a certain class of Americans born at a certain time (regardless of race) *Back to the Future* is a beloved film series because of its endless charm. It's also a tricky series of films that insinuated itself into our consciousness through sly manipulation of nostalgia that seemed so real it must have been created by a time paradox. Today, I hear there's a hoverboard

---

* Weirdly, Sisko's dead wife was also named "Jennifer," and she was featured in at least one time-travelish episode. Luckily, Felecia M. Bell was always able to play her, even when she was an evil Jennifer from an alternate universe.

prototype being tested, as if matching our current technology is just fulfilling *Back to the Future* and not our real future. Which is missing the point really, because I think all this fake nostalgia was more of a series of jokes than anything else, since these movies were comedies above all. The flying-car future was a joke, more of a reference to the 1950s science fiction "golden age" idea of what the future would be like than any sort of "real" future.

Our 2015 is scarily real, while the 2015 of *Back to the Future* was never intended to be any more real than its "past" or "present." Instead, everything that works (and doesn't work) about this pop stalwart does so thanks to fake nostalgia, which really is no different from Doc sticking garbage into the DeLorean to make it fly.

Imagine There's No Frodo
(I Wonder If You Can)

When I was three or so, my parents used to drop me off with a nice Mormon couple who named their daughter "Galadriel," in honor of the beautiful Elf person from *The Lord of the Rings* who we now know looks exactly like Cate Blanchett. In the early '80s, I didn't know what a Mormon was, or who Cate Blanchett was, but I'd like to think that I just inherently understood Elves. Beyond her name, there's not much today that my mother can recall about my Galadriel or her family. They lived close enough to us in Mesa, Arizona, to function as a great place to plop me when my parents both needed to go to the grocery store, mind the fish store they owned together, or, possibly, get high and have sex. Beyond that, nothing has been retained of this friendship other than one Polaroid of the two of us; and I'm clutching the hand of the three-year-old version of the Lady of Lothlorien.

Pronouncing the names of all the characters in *The Lord of the Rings* is tricky enough, but if you're a three-year-old, it's totally impossible. The only thing my mom does remember about little Galadriel turns out to be the best thing: I could not pronounce her name at all. Instead of saying "Galadriel," tiny-me apparently shortened it into a portmanteau word: "Deedle," which rhymes with "needle." This means that I'm the only Tolkien fan to invent my own canonical nickname for one of the major characters, though there are exactly zero references to a "Deedle" in any of the appendices in *The Return of the King.* Can you imagine Ian McKellan's Gandalf saying the word "Deedle"? Do it now, please.

Despite how uncommon this name is, I've been unable to track down my old playmate. Dreamingly, I believe there's an alternate universe where Deedle and I grew up and became great friends and I learned from her—a real-life Galadriel—how to pronounce "Galadriel." As it stands, in this reality, our families drifted apart and Deedle is out there somewhere, a riddle in the dark of my childhood, which is only mildly interesting because I didn't have any other childhood friends with names like Spock or Gizmo. So, I had to learn how to pronounce this name like the rest of you who have read *The Hobbit* or *The Lord of the Rings* trilogy: I invented a pronunciation in my head and then was shocked how wrong I was when the Peter Jackson movies came out in 2001.

In all seriousness, though, I think my toddler-self's apprehension over learning the real pronunciation of "Galadriel" was a prescient metaphor for how afraid I am of real Tolkien fans. They're not a vicious bunch at all, but hard-core Tolkien scholars are patient with information in ways that I am not. They can accept the fact that a whole relationship/marriage can exist as a footnote. They can believe that Tolkien merely "translated" these works from other languages. They can endlessly ponder if the Hobbits are very gay or actually metaphors for Christian values or, possibly, both. Going down the hobbit-hole of Tolkien scholarship is really, really difficult because J. R. R. Tolkien himself was like a built-in scholar/fan of his own work. If Neil deGrasse Tyson were to write science fiction novels, and those novels became immensely popular, I feel like he would become the Tolkien of sci-fi, the inventor of a new genre who is nearly beyond reproach in terms of the logistics of how his fictional world actually functions. In stark opposition to George Lucas—who is clearly unaware of how his fictional world functions—Tolkien is such an expert on his own material that jumping from the frying pan of casual fan to the fire of serious discussion of his work is scary for any serious writer or critic.

Luckily, I'm more of a Bilbo and I'm not serious. I'm a fool. So here we go.

There are numerous ways of thinking about Tolkien's intentions, and a lot of facts and interviews to sort through, but I think even the most hard-core Tolkien scholars will agree with me when I say that *The Lord of the Rings* trilogy only exists because Tolkien's original publisher asked him to write a sequel to *The Hobbit*. In *The Letters of J. R. R. Tolkien*, there's tons of evidence to indicate the author originally had no intention of writing a sequel to *The Hobbit* at all. Specifically, in a 1937 letter to his publisher Stanley Unwin (of Allen & Unwin) Tolkien says, "I am a little perturbed. I cannot think of anything more to say about *hobbits*." This is funny because Tolkien obviously believes it at the time, but the ten-year process of coming around to think the exact opposite is one of the most important retcons in geek history. If Tolkien had continued to respond to letters from fans and his publisher with a similar "no thanks" sentiment, I can't imagine the "fantasy" half of science fiction and fantasy existing in a way that is recognizable at all. The eventual decision Tolkien made to seriously write a "sequel" to *The Hobbit* is the big bang of fantasy, a revolutionary turning point that makes an alternate reality without *The Lord of the Rings* almost impossible to fathom in retrospect, even though it's fascinatingly bizarre that in our universe, any of this happened at all.

John Lennon famously thought "Help!" should be a slow song, which puts him in the genius company of J. R. R. Tolkien, who also didn't initially understand the commercial value of his own work. What I mean is, Tolkien wanted the superboring tome called *The Silmarillion* to come out before *The Hobbit*, and later, as part of *The Lord of the Rings*, though his publisher wouldn't allow it. *The Silmarillion* is also symptomatic of something I like to call the Magician's Nephew Bullshit, insofar as the effect it has on *The Hobbit* and *The Lord of the Rings* is similar to what C. S. Lewis did with the Narnia books. *The Silmarillion* "explains" why the fantasy world of Middle-Earth exists the same way Lewis's *The Magician's Nephew* explains how Narnia became Narnia. Magician's Nephew Bullshit values accuracy over narrative fun. As Laura Miller explains in *The Magician's Book*, "Some lines in *The Lion, the Witch and the Wardrobe* don't make much sense if you presume that its readers are already familiar with *The Magician's Nephew*." This is why there's literally no good reason to read *The Chronicles of Narnia* in anything other than the publication order, and possibly (and controversially) why you never need to read *The Silmarillion*. Magician's Nephew Bullshit totally applies to *Star Wars Episode I: The Phantom Menace*, but you already knew that.

Like George Lucas, Tolkien is an insane historical revisionist of his own work, though—totally unlike Lucas—a wildly successful one. He revised his original 1937 novel *The Hobbit or There and Back Again*, and this revision appeared in 1951.* It differs radically enough from the original to allow *The Lord of the Rings* to exist at all. Specifically, Gollum goes from being a curious creature with funny opinions about things to a straight-up murderous psychopath. Furthermore, the original version of *The Hobbit* doesn't indicate at all that the Ring was bad news. However, try getting your hands on an original 1937 version of *The Hobbit* these days. It's not a conspiracy exactly, but a totally successful retcon. Because Tolkien *revised* that version of *The Hobbit* to make it compatible with *The Lord of the Rings* after the fact, he's totally guilty of Magician's Nephew Bullshit, even though he's one of the only people who ever made it work insofar as it is completely accepted by the fans.

But we need to back up. If *The Hobbit* is the on-accident prequel to *The Lord of the Rings*, what's the big deal? He wrote *The Hobbit*, people liked it, so he wrote a cool series of novels as

* There were two more revised *Hobbit*s, published in 1958 and 1966, respectively. Broadly, they're similar enough to the first revision, at least for our purposes here.

a follow-up. Why would anyone care or think that's profound? Well, if Tolkien hadn't come around to turning his *Hobbit* sequel into *The Lord of the Rings*, fantasy as we know it wouldn't exist because *LOTR* is to fantasy what the Beatles are to rock and roll.

Try to imagine a world without the Beatles. Really, really try. I think there's a very real chance that such a world is a ravaged, burned-out cinder that has a culture not dissimilar to the creepy-melting-faces people who live underneath the Earth in *Beneath the Planet of the Apes*. I can't prove this of course, because there's not a direct correlation between nuclear war being averted and the Beatles releasing "I Want to Hold Your Hand," but still. It's nearly incomprehensible to imagine a contemporary world of pop/rock music without the Beatles, which is partly attributed to Ringo Starr joining the group in 1962. Their original drummer—Pete Best—was infamously unceremoniously fired from the group just prior to the Fabs signing with Brian Epstein and truly becoming a universal phenomenon. If the Beatles didn't chuck Pete Best, they might not have been managed by Brian Epstein, and suddenly, your parents didn't have the right music to listen to and you're not born at all or able to read this book. So, follow this closely: Bilbo is Pete Best and Frodo is Ringo Starr.

Because Bilbo's journey totally concludes arguably even before the end of *The Hobbit*, you couldn't possibly make him the star of *The Hobbit Part 2*, and that's because Bilbo isn't a character who is "part 2" material. You might think Ringo is the everyman of the Beatles, but that's because he's the everyman who went on the adventure and *stayed* on the adventure.

Bilbo's the guy who went on the journey and came back again and stayed home, like Pete Best. Bilbo is an intentionally and aggressively unremarkable everyman whose hero's journey is so anticonformist punk rock that he actually doesn't do much traditional heroic stuff in the last section of *The Hobbit*. In a 1975 essay called "The Psychological Journey of Bilbo Baggins," Dorothy Matthews asserts: "It stands to reason that Tolkien does not have Bilbo kill the dragon because that would be more the deed of a savior or culture hero, such as St. George, or the Red Cross Knight, or Beowulf. The significance of this tale lies in the very obvious anti-heroic manner in which Tolkien chooses to bring Bilbo's adventures to a conclusion."

Sitting out the big battles and not taking a lot of credit make Bilbo the star of an epic adventure who doesn't act like the star. So, when *The Hobbit* demanded a sequel, Tolkien needed something old (a Hobbit) and something new, and what we got out of that equation was Frodo Baggins, Bilbo's plucky nephew, a deeper kind of Magician's Nephew Bullshit that is actually not bullshit.

If viewed through the lens of heroic archetypes, in every way, Bilbo is a more iconoclastic character than Frodo, because he actively protests being part of the story that he's in. Frodo isn't nearly as iconoclastic, and structurally, the narrative style of *The Lord of the Rings* is a little more efficient than that of *The Hobbit*. I know, I sound like a crazy person: a three-novel trilogy is somehow more efficient in its language than a tiny little three-hundred-page deal called *The Hobbit*. I'm totally nuts. But I'm not. *The Lord of the Rings* books are way more plot oriented than the meandering child's journey of *The Hobbit*. In

"Narrative Pattern in *The Fellowship of the Ring*," David M. Miller talks about picturesque writing versus writing that focuses on the movement of the ring. He argues that with a few exceptions (like Tom Bombadil) everything that happens in *The Lord of the Rings* is answering the main plot question of WHERE IS THE RING NOW?

Meanwhile, there's a lot of random shit in *The Hobbit*— goblin attack, giant spiders, lots of eating and singing—not all of which really adds up to an exciting plot, which is exactly why turning this book into a series of three films was a great idea for making money for New Line Cinema, but a terrible idea in terms of making watchable movies. The characters in *The Hobbit* are forced in their film adaptations to sustain themselves over narrative distances they were not designed to cross. Peter Jackson tried to turn *The Hobbit* into *The Lord of the Rings* when he made his film adaptations of the novel, and if J. R. R. Tolkien had attempted the inverse—to make *The Lord of the Rings* a true sequel to *The Hobbit*—nobody would have liked *The Lord of the Rings*.

The creation of *The Lord of the Rings* is Tolkien, effectively, and brilliantly, *selling out*, which is exactly like the Beatles firing Pete Best. What was it like inside of Tolkien's brain when he decided he needed a more traditional hero like Frodo? Let's take a speculative peek into his thought process:

> You know what? I can't have a series of epic novels with some potbellied loser at the center of the action. Who's going to read all that crap? No one! I need a similar dude, only younger and, you know, fuck it, *cooler*

than Bilbo. It will be his nephew. That's good. Frodo. Fine. Good. Done. He's got a Hobbit friend, too. Wait. Screw that, he's got THREE friends. They'll all be a little like Bilbo, only younger and drunker. They're like a band. I love this. I'm a genius. What else?

I also need some straight-up cold, hard badasses, too. Shit. Well, I've got Gandalf, so I'll make him even more of a bad motherfucker than last time. Maybe I'll even kill him and have him come back to life like a massive player. Yeah, everyone will love that. Hell, *I* love that. I'm Tolkien and I love Christian metaphors. Wow. C. S. Lewis is going to be soooo pissed. Aslan coming back in the same novel is going to be such a joke compared to when I bring back Gandalf in *The Two Towers*. Ha-ha. Take that C. S.! I'll show you who wins the war of the dudes with initials who write amazing books. Okay.

Anyway. Back to cold, hard badassess. Who else? I know, I'll get a guy, a regular guy, who wears *shoes*, and I'll name him Strider. But later, his name will be something else. Everybody has multiple names. Just like me. Cause I'm J. R. R. Tolkien.

From here, you can do your own Elvish translation of "dropping the mic."

Now, the three Hobbit films—*An Unexpected Journey, The Desolation of Smaug,* and *Misty Mountain Hop**—benefit from

---

* I know "The Battle of the Five Armies" is in the book, but using it as the subtitle of the movie, when they had a perfectly good subtitle—"There and Back Again," which is the actual subtitle of the book—is just baffling. For now, I'll only call this movie *Misty Mountain Hop*, because I hate the

the fact that most people who like the books would never say the film version of *The Lord of the Rings* trilogy "ruined" the book version of *The Lord of the Rings* trilogy. And it's also impossible to ruin *The Hobbit*, because nobody cares about it the way they care about *The Lord of the Rings*, because in comparison, it's just not as good. "Good," however, is not the same as funny or relevant, because if *The Hobbit* hadn't been as funny and as interesting as it was (revised version or not), there's no way the rest of this would have happened. And that impact is obviously dramatic in the existence of the fantasy genre as we know it. A lot of people might not see this in a positive light: writer Michael Moorcock, for instance, who once "took down" Tolkien by comparing the series to A. A. Milne in an essay called "Epic Pooh." Why being compared to an awesome writer like A. A. Milne is a takedown is confusing to me; plus even if fantasy writers want to write differently than Tolkien (like Moorcock) they're still acknowledging his influence. Could anyone write a Christmas story without at least thinking about Dickens and ghosts post *A Christmas Carol*? Did Dickens "ruin" Christmas as a result?

The alternate universe without Tolkien's accidental Hobbit sequel, *The Lord of the Rings*, is one without Star Wars and Harry Potter, and one with much stricter antimarijuana laws. This book trilogy normalized the idea of wizards sacrificing themselves (à la Obi-Wan Kenobi and Dumbledore) and also featured literally all

---

"real" title so much. For comparison of just how annoying I am, I also irrationally call the American version of *The Office* "The Fake Office."

of its characters toking up before a big adventure. The fact that dorm rooms in the '60s and '70s frequently bore a map of Middle-Earth isn't just because people wanted to live in Middle-Earth, but because people in college like to get high, and a lot of that is in the DNA—accidental or not—of *The Lord of the Rings*. Appropriately enough, "pipe weed" doesn't show up in *The Hobbit* as much, because, you know, little kids shouldn't smoke pot.

◆

In 2001, I'm sitting in my room in a house in Mesa, Arizona, which I'm renting for $200 a month. My landlord is a toothless Gollum, a guy who actually sleeps in a bed in the backyard and never wears shoes despite the fact that he drives only rented Lincoln Town Cars. There's no way this guy was doing anything legal to get himself in this situation, and like Gollum, a fallen Hobbit, my landlord seemed to have been once great, but now was consumed by some evil and terrible addiction/affliction that made him into a weirdo. Of course, I have zero sympathy for that because I'm twenty years old and living in my own rented room, paging through a dog-eared copy of *The Fellowship of the Ring*, waiting for my friends to arrive so we can drive over to the movie theatre and see the first *Lord of the Rings* movie for the first time, at midnight. If you've been reading these essays in order, you'll know there's a weird tradition among my friends and me for pulling jerky stunts at midnight premieres of big geek movies, and the premiere of *The Fellowship of the Ring* in 2001 was the first and the oddest.

It goes without saying that if your landlord sleeps in the

backyard and wears no shoes and is a secret criminal, people don't ring the doorbell of your house but, rather, just let themselves in. In certain parts of Mesa, Arizona, it's *Breaking Bad* all the time. So, when I hear a tremendous bellow, "The wizards have arrived!" I sort of know what is up. My best friends, Billy and George, have let themselves into my house and they are in costume, ready for the premiere. The thing is, they aren't dressed as any real characters from *The Lord of the Rings* but, instead, as generic, ridiculous, off-the-rack wizards sporting polyester robes and Prince Valiant–style bobs. There were pinks and periwinkles pervading these robes, and ironed-on flames and half-crescent moons. These characters' self-proclaimed names were "Wizard Fro-Ty" and "Wizard Irwin." George had never read a lick of Tolkien, and Billy was a bigger fan than I was, yet both had conspired to create intentionally stupid wizard costumes to wear to go see the movie. I hung my head in shame as we squeezed into my pickup truck for the fifteen-minute drive to the multiplex.

Of course, everyone who camped out for the movie *hated* these fake wizards, which didn't stop George and Billy from "casting hexes" on random strangers or chanting out nonsense incantations to spells that weren't "real." If you've ever seen footage of Triumph the Insult Comic Dog screwing with people in line for *Star Wars*, this was a little like that. Also, the "George Lucas Is a Virgin" thing we pulled a few years later was tame compared to this, because George and Billy in their colorful, foppish wizard robes were actually torturing real Gandalfs and Aragorns. In what can only be called Y2K geek-smack-talk, I heard many of the costumed Elves and Hobbits in line murmur, "These guys look more like Harry Potter fans. What losers!"

The culmination of George and Billy's evil scheme happened when the local news station showed up to report on all the Tolkien fans lined up for the first *Lord of the Rings* movie and they interviewed George and Billy *instead* of the "real" fans. They were funnier, they were more flamboyant, they filled the stereotype of what the newspeople were looking for, people who also had probably never read a lick of Tolkien. My mom even managed to catch some of this action on a VHS tape she kept handy for whenever someone we knew (occasionally me) idiotically showed up on the local news for being ridiculous.

Here's the scary thing: if Tolkien had never written his sequel to *The Hobbit*, if he'd never decided that Gollum was an addict and fallen monster, if he'd never sold out and created a more mainstream hero in the form of Frodo, if it had all just been *The Hobbit*, the wizards you would see in line for a "geek" movie would still only be the fake ones that George and Billy created for their prank. Unwittingly, my friends were drawing on signals from an alternate dimension where fantasy never got a hold of itself and never began to take itself seriously. Their faux wizards are straight from a dimension that none of us thankfully will ever have to live in. A world where Gandalf isn't as famous, and Frodo doesn't exist.

Regeneration No. 9

Living in Manhattan on unemployment payments from the government will teach you obvious lessons about financial responsibility as it relates to the rising cost of forty-ounce beers, but it will also show you just how badly you manage your time. You without a job is who you really are and if you don't like that person you've got to figure out how to change that. In February 2008, I was subletting an apartment smack in the middle of Manhattan, barely scraping by on unemployment, and slowly losing my shit. In New York City the word "slowly" means "quickly," because we've scientifically figured out that time passes more egregiously here. In lots of sci-fi stories, people will seem to rapidly age because time has been sped up or slowed down. This is what it's like to crack up in New York.

After being laid off from a cool restaurant job that I liked, and teetering on the brink of endless ennui over an on-again, off-again long-distance relationship with a painter, my dour mood wasn't helped by the fact that I was watching a ton of *Battlestar Galactica*. Like many of you, I'm fully aware that *BSG* was/is one of the best things to happen to science fiction on television, and endless discussion over who the final Cylon was certainly birthed niche websites dedicated exclusively to geek discussion.* But it's also a fact that *Battlestar Galactica* is depressing as hell, particularly in season four. What passes for humor or upbeat moments on *BSG* is the equivalent of the soldiers whistling at the beginning of *The Bridge on the River Kwai*.† I'm not saying it isn't a great show—it really is—it's just that watching Admiral Adama drink himself silly and CRY because the *Galactica* rolled up on a fake version of Earth full of robot skeletons wasn't doing much for my job search, nor was the dark nebula of mush spreading out in my brain. Now, enter *Doctor Who*, and the David Tennant era that totally saved my life.

My father, of course, had tried to sic '70s and '80s *Doctor Who* on me when I was growing up, but back then, I was like most pre-2005 American "classic" *Doctor Who* fans: I had no idea what was going on in any given episode. If you've already read about my childhood experiences with *Barbarella*, then you can guess what my dad's angle was on the Tom Baker incarnation of *Doctor Who*. Hint: it wasn't the long scarf or the robot dog. Old-school *Doctor Who* may not have been able to compete with old-school *Star Trek* in the pointless half-naked

---

* My alma mater, Tor.com, and *Gawker*'s geek empire, *io9*, were both launched in 2008.

† Unrelated, but I love reminding people that the other big novel that Pierre Boulle wrote other than *The Bridge over the River Kwai* was *Planet of the Apes*. Seriously, I will never shut up about this when people mention *Kwai*, *Apes*, David Lean, or, occasionally, Alec Guinness.

women department, but with costars like Leela (Louise Jameson) and later Peri (Nicola Bryant) it certainly tried. I've been heartened to learn that contemporary *Doctor Who* scholars refer to those characters dismissively as "for the dads."

So, before becoming aware of the new *Doctor Who* in 2005, I was among the vast majority of American sci-fi fans who believed that the character's name wasn't "the Doctor," but instead "Dr. Who,"* and that he was a weird guy with a giant scarf who fought obnoxious robots called Daleks, who in turn looked like big versions of R2-D2 crossed with toilet implements.

Streaming video still sort of sucked in 2008, and getting *Doctor Who* on cable was pretty hard. Luckily, the whole show up through season three was on Netflix, which meant if I ordered the discs I'd have some kind of new sci-fi show to fill the time between drinking too much and watching a new episode of *Battlestar* in which everyone was drinking too much. Right away, it didn't quite work—because the 2005 *Doctor Who* relaunch with Christopher Eccleston didn't really do it for me. He wore a leather jacket. He lectured poor Rose (Billie Piper) about how dumb she was. He randomly called human beings apes. It was jerky and too English, even for me. Still, I got an education. I learned that the faux-R2-D2 things—the

---

* To be fair, this is confusing, and ironically arch in only a way that the British could be capable of. It's made even more confusing by the fact that there are weird remake movies in the '80s in which the character is played by Peter Cushing (Tarkin in Star Wars!) and is actually named "Dr. Who." Obviously the Cushing "Dr. Who" films, *Dr. Who and the Daleks* and *Daleks—Invasion Earth: 2150 A.D.*, don't count as part of the real *Doctor Who* canon, but their existence prior to the current popularity of the "real" show certainly helps excuse why the character's name—or lack thereof—is confusing for the uninitiated.

Daleks—weren't actually robots at all, but rather mutated cyborg combos, and that despite not loving the Doctor himself, the show was somehow the most progressive thing I'd ever seen. Much has been written about Captain Jack Harkness (John Barrowman), the dashing pansexual badass who joins the Doctor and Rose for the second half of the first season, and count me among those who were floored by how much I wasn't floored when Captain Jack planted dual nonbinary smooches on both Rose and the Doctor. This weird sci-fi show was doing way more for sexual politics than *Battlestar* was, that was for sure.*

Just because something is aligned with your politics doesn't mean it's automatically your favorite TV show, and even though I *liked* the first season of *Doctor Who*, Eccleston's Doctor (whom I totally adore now) was too much of a downer for me. Commiserating with sci-fi and fantasy survivors is a normal part of loving these kinds of big heroes (Batman's parents get shot, Luke Skywalker's house is burned down, Dorothy Gale is caught in a tornado and accidentally becomes a murderer), but Eccleston's Ninth Doctor couldn't bring me out of the sad stupor I was wallowing in. However, when he randomly became a TOTALLY DIFFERENT PERSON in the first season finale, "The Parting of the Ways," I actually screamed with joy. The *Doctor Who* notion of regeneration—the idea that the hero can become a new person—is profound likely because it's a hyperbolic inversion of how people desperately try to affect real change in their own lives.

---

* Read *Queers Dig Time Lords* (Mad Norwegian Press, 2013) for tons of excellent exploration of gender politics in *Doctor Who* and its spin-offs.

At this point, for those who really still don't know what *Doctor Who* is or what the hell I'm talking about, here's a brief primer. In 1963, the world (mostly the British) got its first taste of a guy named the Doctor, an irascible old man, played by William Hartnell, who turns out to be a centuries-old alien capable of traveling in time and space using a machine called the TARDIS, which stands for "Time and Relative Dimension in Space." This time machine/spaceship is shaped like a 1950s police telephone box, because it has a gizmo that allows it to blend into its surroundings. BUT, because that gizmo also got broken, the blue police box just looks like a police box on the outside. On the inside, it's way bigger, because of sci-fi magic, making it more like the inside of Mary Poppins's bag than a real-deal Star Wars spaceship.* From the beginning, the Doctor is a kooky, non-machismo, nonviolent, brainy hero. He's more Sherlock Holmes than James Bond, but kinder than both. And unlike both Bond and Holmes, when this character needed to be played by a different actor, there was an actual in-universe explanation.

When William Hartnell became too frail to play the Doctor and was replaced by the actor Patrick Troughton, the writers decided that they'd actually explain why the character looked different.† In fact, they also decided to explain why he *acted*

---

* Donna Noble gets a good dig in about this fact in "Planet of the Ood," when, seeing another, more traditional spaceship, she exclaims, "A real proper rocket! Now that's what I call a spaceship. You've got a box, he's got a Ferrari."

† This episode was part of a serial called *The Tenth Planet*, written by Kit Pedler and Gerry Davis. The entire story is actually "missing," meaning you can't watch the whole thing, which is tragically true of a lot of early *Doctor Who* recordings. Meanwhile, *Doctor Who* itself was created by Verity

different. Because he was a Time Lord alien from the planet Gallifrey, he would *change* into a new person, also called "the Doctor," who would retain all the previous Doctor's memories, but be a totally new man. There have been thirteen Doctors since the transition from Hartnell to Troughton and as the show progressed, this process was branded as "regeneration." The regeneration episodes of any era of *Doctor Who* always are among the biggest and most emotional for the fans and are also really odd for someone unfamiliar with the show.* Protagonists with the ability to hit the reset button, presumably even on their gender,† are a bizarre narrative phenomenon in any fiction and, as far as I know, totally unique to *Doctor Who.*

Controversially, Christopher Eccleston only did one season of the *Doctor Who* reboot, so right away, *new* fans the

---

Lambert and Sydney Newman just prior to 1962. There's a lot of history to delve into here, but the fact that Verity Lambert was a woman in a male-dominated industry, partly responsible for creating an iconic and enduring and primarily *nonviolent* sci-fi TV show, is something everyone should remind everyone all the time. The 2013 TV movie *An Adventure in Time and Space*, though it takes some broad liberties with history, is a heartwarming, must-watch docudrama about the early days of the show. In fact, if you've never seen *Doctor Who*, it's not a bad place to start.

* People freaked out about this—crying fits and everything—particularly when Tennant left. My friend Emily Asher-Perrin wrote an essay about this called "When Your Doctor Is No Longer the Doctor: How to Survive Regeneration" for Tor.com in December 2013, right before Matt Smith left. It's tops.

† The contemporary version of the show has outright established that Time Lords can and do regenerate into other genders. The Master, the long-running male nemesis of the Doctor, returned in the eighth season, in 2014, as Michelle Gomez's "the Mistress," or "Missy." The old show used to call female Time Lords like Romana (Mary Tamm; post-regeneration, Lalla Ward) "Time Ladies." Every day on the Internet, everyone (including myself) asks if the Doctor will ever become one. My personal vote for a future lady-Doctor is Michelle Dockery.

world over experienced not only their first Doctor but also their first regeneration episode. After taking on the Daleks and absorbing the time vortex (there are lots of vortices in *Doctor Who*), the Doctor is exhausted and explains to his friend Rose (standing in for the audience) that he's going to "change." It's a great and touching moment, and just as Eccleston delivers his catchphrase "fantastic," golden light shoots from his neck and arms and BAM, he's got funky hair, and he's David Tennant! I was shocked, a little irritated, but, most of all, excited. How could this be? Could this show be getting happy? Was there hope for all of us?

The answer was a hysterical yes, because Tennant's portrayal of the Doctor (at least in his first few seasons) is not a downer at all. With his skinny suits, insane hair, manic hand gestures, and Chuck Taylor sneakers, this version of the Doctor was a full-on space hipster, but without the depressing irony. For me, sitting alone in a cold Manhattan sublet, wondering what I was going to do with my life, fighting whatever version of depression everyone in their twenties is stricken with, the new Doctor was a revelation. I wore Chuck Taylors and a suit jacket, *too*. I liked jazzy one-liners and over-the-top exclamations of approval, *too*. Within a week, *Doctor Who* had me going from the "oh no" inside my head to the "OHHHH YES!" of David Tennant. I was putting on my Chucks and leaving the house more often, drinking less, looking for new work, taking my writing more seriously. *Doctor Who*'s reboot to Tennant showed me that one of the most embarrassing clichés about life can be true: when one door closes, another one opens.

Plus, I was still two seasons behind, and everyone knows

binge-watching anything awesome coupled with a new sense of purpose is like having a placebo-epiphany every forty-five minutes. I'm not sure if therapists should prescribe binge-watching, but in this case, it worked for me.

Where there had been angst with Christopher Eccleston's Doctor, it felt unearned, because the new audience hadn't been through anything with him, as we didn't see his home planet Gallifrey destroyed in a giant war.* But if you became a convert to *Doctor Who* just before the David Tennant era, then you felt like you'd already suffered something with him: you remembered when he was Eccleston! And you got to mourn the loss of that identity with him because in Tennant's first proper episode, "The Christmas Invasion," he has to convince British prime minister Harriet Jones (Penelope Wilton)† that he is the same man as Christopher Eccleston, and it's mad painful, because you both love this new Doctor and, weirdly, miss the older, grumpier one. And by the end of his first season, the brilliant showrunner Russell T. Davies hit his stride of tugging on your heartstrings‡ by banishing the Doctor's girlfriend/best

---

* BUT, when we did get to "see" the Time War in various episodes, most notably "The Day of the Doctor," it didn't do much for giving us feelings, mostly because the Time Lords seemed so generic and white. Still, it did do a better job than, say, showing us why Anakin Skywalker fell to the Dark Side of the Force during the Clone Wars. Some wars, whether they be Clone or Time, should stay offscreen.

† Also known as Matthew Crawley's mother on *Downton Abbey*.

‡ Prior to *Doctor Who*, Davies was most famous for creating the original version of *Queer as Folk*. Current showrunner Steven Moffat wrote and created the show *Coupling* before being placed in charge of *Doctor Who*, following Davies's departure, which coincided with Tennant's. Davies is still remembered fondly among fans for his twenty-first-century progressive politics, whereas Steven Moffat has rapidly become the George Lucas of *Doctor Who*, an embarrassing dad whom we love because, you know, we have to.

friend Rose Tyler to an alternate dimension, reminding all of us that just because you get a new lease on life and intentionally become happier, bad stuff (Cybermen) can still happen.

The next two and a half seasons of David Tennant's tenure find him perpetrating unrequited love by ignoring the eye-batting of poor Martha Jones (Freema Agyeman), as well as meeting old enemies and making a new BFF in the form of Donna Noble, played wonderfully by Catherine Tate.* *Doctor Who*'s formula almost always has included a "companion" in the form of a woman who hangs out with the Doctor for reasons that are often dubious, confusing, and, occasionally, offensive. Tate's Donna Noble remains, to this day, *Who*'s masterstroke of how you can invert expectations and create a lasting and interesting character dynamic. Donna and the Doctor don't have romantic tension and are in essence a comedy duo.† I watched Donna's season (season four) in real time in 2008, because I was caught up by that point, and it is still my personal favorite run of all of *Doctor Who*. The message to me was simple: you

---

* David Tennant did three full seasons (a season is called a "series" in England) of *Doctor Who*, which in the context of the relaunched show are seasons two through four. However, because he was playing Hamlet for the Royal Shakespeare Company, he created a long swan song from *Doctor Who* by doing four stand-alone episodes from 2009 to 2010 that were a little longer and ended in his regeneration episode, "The End of Time, Part 2." These are either considered "the specials" or part of season four. When Matt Smith became the Doctor in "The End of Time, Part 2," Smith's subsequent season was referred to as season (or "series") FIVE exclusively. Tennant of course came back in 2013 for the "Day of the Doctor" anniversary episode, which combined with his "half" season makes it seem like he was in the role for longer than he really was.

† Though, after both left *Doctor Who*, Tennant and Tate played Benedick and Beatrice in a run of Shakespeare's rom-com *Much Ado About Nothing* on the West End in London.

might change your whole life and lose love, but real good friends are REALLY fucking hard to come by, specifically if you live a life of intergalactic adventure.

✦

There have been two Doctors since David Tennant: Matt Smith and the current guy, Peter Capaldi. The regeneration of the Doctor into a new person every few years is brilliant primarily because it removes a sense of ego from the character and the show. Sure, we've had a lot of guys play Batman over the years, but that's a character hiding behind a mask. Plus, with TV shows it's different. A sitcom called *Frasier* wouldn't work if suddenly a new person showed up to play Frasier or if Frasier regenerated into a new radio shrink, who is now inexplicably played by Gilbert Gottfried. Yet, this is exactly what *Doctor Who* does; it shakes things up often, and adapts and evolves and changes each time it does so. Sometimes these changes are slight and safe. (The Doctors played by David Tennant and his successor, Matt Smith, aren't *that* different.) And sometimes they're very different. (Incumbent Doctor Peter Capaldi is waaaay different from anyone they've had since 2005.) Still, because it's a different actor, the change is radical, and yet, the audience is supposed to believe this is the same person, even though he looks and acts totally different.

I think this gives me and other *Doctor Who* fans strong feelings, because it's the opposite of real life. In real life, we change, but we essentially look the same. The Doctor is the reverse because he "stays the same," but looks and acts differently. His soul is saved, and his memories of a past life are intact, but he can move on from the baggage of that past life, totally forgiven and literally reborn. The Christ metaphors here are a bit obvious, because the Doctor often "dies" in saving everyone and, in Tennant's case, holds his arms out like he's being crucified in "The End of Time."

And yet, I think the regeneration process is more interesting if we think of it like the end of a relationship. Like a breakup. You don't die in a breakup, but it certainly feels that way. You have good memories of the other person, but also of *who you were* in that relationship. The Doctor, in essence, breaks up with himself every time he regenerates, and as our hearts are broken by his departure, he immediately rebounds with a new person, who is also *him*. It's no wonder that in the fictional reality of *Doctor Who*, his alien anatomy includes two hearts: one for now, one for later.

Right before his regeneration scene in 2013's "The Time of the Doctor," Matt Smith's bow-tie-wearing Doctor (an even bigger hipster than David Tennant) says, "We all change. When you think about it, we're all different people, all through our lives. But that's okay, you gotta keep moving, so long as you remember all the people that you used to be." This is a mirror of how we actually live our lives, how we actually let go of our past selves, by paradoxically always honoring them by talking about our past constantly. In this way, *Doctor Who*'s regeneration process should be required viewing for anyone trying to write a memoir. Or at the very least, anyone who writes *about* writing about memoir. David Shields, I'm waiting by my phone(box): have you seen *Doctor Who*?

Over the years, since becoming a more "professional" *Doctor*

Who fan, I've been crankier about the specific ins and outs of the show than I was after I experienced that first regeneration. At any comic con, you'll see hundreds of people wearing a popular T-shirt that declares "You Never Forget Your First Doctor," and I think I'll amend that to say, "You never forget the first Doctor whom you regenerated with." Even though he wasn't Tennant, I grew to love Tennant's younger (my exact age) successor, Matt Smith, but maybe not because of anything Smith did specifically. In 2010, during another moment of change and reinvention in my life—this time the end of a relationship and the start of a new job—Matt Smith's Doctor presented me with a kind of emotional ultimatum: Are you going to let go of David Tennant or not? Are you so committed to the past that you can't move forward?

I've never owned a bow tie, but at the time, PRIOR to the commencement of the Matt Smith era, I was regularly rocking his signature tweed jacket with elbow patches. It goes without saying that people have assumed I wear Chuck Taylors or tweed jackets because I'm a *Doctor Who* fan, and though I used to correct them, pointing out that I was into Chucks and tweed *before* Matt Smith and Tennant, I don't anymore. One of the nice things about *Doctor Who* is that it makes sneakers into space shoes, bow ties into a badge of heroism, and fairly ordinary jackets into the costume of a superhero. In the season eight finale, "Death in Heaven," in-universe *Doctor Who* fandom representative Osgood (Ingrid Oliver) mashes up Smith and Tennant by rocking both a bow tie and red Chucks, reminding me, like a good memoir, of who the Doctor used to be, this time reflected in the face of a fan. Fans of *Doctor Who* are often quite different from fans of any other big geeky thing, and that's because the pain of constant change is woven into a zany science fiction epic starring a person who wears clothes just like yours.

If *Doctor Who* were a real-life memoir, we'd maybe be members of the Doctor's faux family, who also don't know if we are the Doctor himself. Will we become our parents and mentors? Will they become us? Have they already?

No, Luke, *Captain Kirk* Is Your Father

Asking me if I like Star Trek is like asking a Muslim if it's fun to celebrate Ramadan. I can't remember a time when Star Trek wasn't in my vocabulary, and in discussing favorite TV shows on the playground in 1991 I'd always say "*Star Trek* is my favorite, but not *the new one*." Why was I snobby about *The Next Generation*? As a ten-year-old no less! It wasn't that I didn't like and respect *The Next Generation*; it just wasn't the exact religion I belonged to. There are a lot of different kinds of Christians, and there are lots of different kinds of Star Trek people.

This isn't to say that there was any kind of obsessive trek-kie mania in my house. My father's La-Z-Boy wasn't converted to resemble Captain Kirk's command chair, and my parents didn't dress up me and my sister in Klingon costumes. And even though I was alone in being into the toys and collectibles for a little bit, like everybody else I wasn't *that* devout. Star Trek was like a religion in my house, but *not* because of rituals or beliefs. Instead, knowledge of classic *Star Trek* was just a *given*. If my Catholic friends knew how to cross themselves after saying grace through sheer instinct, my sister and I knew to give the Vulcan "Live Long and Prosper" hand gesture as a quick sign of friendship. It was natural in my family to mention the term "mind-meld" at the dinner table, and after a long day teaching elementary school children it wasn't uncommon for my mom to say that she was "on impulse power" while flopping onto the couch and further explaining that her "dilithium crystals were running low." Real religion is about jargon and comfort, which is what it's like to really love Star Trek.

Looking at Star Trek as a half-assed religion makes it easier for me to justify why I often feel like I'm the only person I know who "gets it." Even in geek circles, there's an annoyingly disproportionate amount of attention paid to the 1979–91 classic Star Trek films, specifically to 1982's *The Wrath of Khan*. Everyone will tell you it's the best Star Trek movie, and they are correct. However, *The Wrath* doesn't achieve this status simply because there's lots of shooting or things blowing up or Kirk yelling "KHAAANNN!!!!" or even because Spock gets fake killed. The real reason why *The Wrath* is so baller is because it incorporates classic literature into the basic themes of the story.

Kirk and Spock are quoting Dickens—specifically *A Tale of Two Cities*—throughout this movie, and Khan is quoting Melville's *Moby-Dick*. Every two years in New York City, there's a Moby-Dick Marathon I attend (and once read in), and I swear to God, someone always turns to me and silently mouths the word "Khan!" during the "From Hell's Heart I Stab at Thee!" chase section of the book. Star Trek loves *Moby-Dick* so much that the only good *Next Generation* movie—1996's *First Contact*—even made Captain Picard more legit by having *him* do an Ahab speech and asserting the whole movie, like *Wrath of Khan*, as a sci-fi *Moby-Dick* homage. Captain Janeway, of the super-underrated *Star Trek: Voyager*, dons shades of Ahab on more than one occasion. In "Equinox," Janeway is so pissed at an immoral fellow Starfleet captain that she nearly gets her whole crew turned against her in her quest for quasi revenge. In the finale to the entire series, "Endgame," Janeway pulls a sort of time-travel Ahab thing by attempting to rewrite her own history by destroying her own White Whale, the Borg Queen.

Moby-Dick connections in Star Trek probably come from the episode "The Doomsday Machine," in which the *Enterprise* encounters Captain Matt Decker, whose entire crew was killed by a humongous space critter that looked like a cornucopia. This guy goes from being a crying mess to taking over the *Enterprise* in a psychopathic minute. Star Trek has a lot of captains and a lot of ships, so the nautical connections and essential roles of the characters naturally allow for Ahab to surface constantly. Writer/director Nicholas Meyer was smart enough not only to inject Herman Melville stuff into *The Wrath of Khan*, but also to loosely base the whole naval tone of that film on C. S. Forester's Horatio Hornblower novels. This is also why the J. J. Abrams–directed 2013 film, *Star Trek into Darkness*, sucks. There's no literature in it! From naming one of its goofiest episodes, "This Side of Paradise," after F. Scott Fitzgerald, to quoting Shakespeare constantly, even bad Star Trek is elevated by its use of classic literature. Like his successor Captain Picard,

Captain Kirk has also been into the classics and specifically Shakespeare since way back. The original series episode "The Conscience of the King" arguably kicks off the whole Star Trek tradition of hitting the books and being obsessed with showing you how much everyone on the show cares about reading.* It would be a little reductive to say good Star Trek only works when it's got old-school Western literature cropping up, and that's not really what I mean. Instead, this sort of literary stuff is a positive symptom of when Star Trek is at its best self. Good Star Trek equals soul-searching about the basic nature of humanity, which occasionally means the writing will stray toward famous literature.

In a terrible episode of *The Next Generation* called "Hide and Q," a pre-bearded Commander Riker is tempted with godlike powers by the flippantly omnipotent multidimensional being known only as "Q." Q jerkily taunts Captain Picard about the fragility and pointlessness of human beings, which gives Picard the opportunity to do his favorite thing when someone disagrees with him: channel Shakespeare. Picard delivers the "what a piece of work is man?" speech from *Hamlet* and turns it into a heroic rebuttal. In the *Hamlet* context, "what a piece of work is man?" and its following lines aren't necessarily heroic, but with Picard, the speech becomes something different. This is at the core of Star Trek's successful relationship with literature; even in a bad Star Trek thing, it doesn't copy or pay homage

---

* This is a Star Trek episode with almost no science fiction in it at all, other than the fact that it's set on a spaceship. It's a murder mystery that features a company of Shakespearean players who are hanging out on the *Enterprise*.

poorly; it translates the themes and references creatively. The spin Star Trek puts on literature is inherently a pop one and not entirely dissimilar from a rapper "sampling" a line from another (usually older) artist. When Puff Daddy appropriated the melody of the Police's "I'll Be Watching You" for "I'll Be Missing You," the meaning of the original song was changed. While this is a fairly radical change, I don't think it's that different from Picard turning Hamlet's sad-sack speech into something of a galvanizing cry for why humans rock.

Khan is initially a huge fan of Milton's *Paradise Lost* in "Space Seed," but he switches to Melville in *The Wrath of Khan*. As Khan dies he recites a version of Ahab's "From hell's heart, I stab at thee!" speech. But instead of the tragic aspect of the original text, the sideways appropriation of Melville is what makes Khan more delusional and sympathetic. And that's because Kirk is not the White Whale, and he did not wound Khan specifically the way Moby-Dick wounded Ahab. By making "the White Whale" a person, and "Ahab" even more delusional, these words from *Moby-Dick* take on a mixed-analogous meaning from their source. Ditto for *The Wrath*'s use of *A Tale of Two Cities* throughout. If Dickens's Sydney Carton is a stand-in for Kirk at the beginning of the film—asshole-ish and confused—then Spock is Carton at the end: heroic, humble, and dead. Just in case you missed all of this, *The Wrath of Khan* practically begins with Kirk fumbling through "It was the best of times, it was the worst of times" and ends with him doing the trademark halted William Shatner I'm-just-discovering-these-words-as-they're-coming-to-me rendition of "It is a far,

far better thing THAT I do than I have ever done before. A far better resting place . . . that I go to . . . than . . . I have ever known."*

We already know Star Trek's main competitor, Star Wars, doesn't have any of its characters reading or talking about books,† but how does Star Wars do in terms of books being referenced or paid homage? Well, we're pretty much stuck with stuff like Homer, the Bible, and—all together now—anything Joseph Campbell talks about in *The Hero with a Thousand Faces*. Fans and scholars of Star Wars have for decades now loved to point out that Jungian archetypes present in Star Wars are right in line with Joseph Campbell's theories about the hero's journey. This is why Star Wars is genius and prophetic and why we're in love with it. Everyone is right about this, but because it's so obvious and can be explained so quickly—we're predisposed psychologically to like Star Wars—it's no longer profound or interesting. It's a self-fulfilling statement that ends a conversation instead of beginning one. Because what gets missed in noticing the Jungian stuff in Star Wars is the conclusion that Star Wars films (at least the classic films) are *easy* to like. We tend to all say we like *The Empire Strikes Back* best of all the Star Wars films because, as smarty-pants readers, we know that it's uncool to like a piece of narrative art that has a happy ending. This argument falls apart pretty quickly if we

---

* This quote is a little bit different than it is in the novel. Kirk turns "rest" into "resting place." Similarly when Picard quotes *Moby-Dick* in *First Contact* he says "if his chest were a *cannon*," which is a change from the book's "if his chest were a *mortar*." I guess we can excuse these guys because it's the twenty-third and twenty-fourth century respectively?

† See the title essay of this book, "Luke Skywalker Can't Read."

consider all the *Star Wars* prequels are total downers, but they're downers for different reasons: they're bad movies.*

The religious lip service in Star Wars is so obvious that it really indicates that there's not a real religion there. The spirituality of Star Wars is a stand-in for whatever you feel like inserting into it. The Force is a catchall New Age Spiritualism, made vague enough to make you feel good about it, and cool enough to be an awesome plot device allowing the main characters to perform bona fide feats of full-on magic. The vagueness and generalness of Star Wars is its primary strength, and if you think I'm wrong, consider this: the prequels are regarded as bad for a lot of reasons, but one reason everyone agrees on is that "explaining" a technical aspect of the Force almost ruins it. The details of Star Wars—both moral and technical—are not as important as the broad strokes or swipes of the lightsaber. Star Wars presents simple answers—or at the very least *allegories*—to the problems of life. I'm not saying Star Wars is dumbed-down storytelling, but if Star Wars is like Homer—epic, moving, and distant—then Star Trek is more like Dickens. In short, Star Trek is about flawed humans while Star Wars is about gods.

The stories of Star Trek are never focused on trying to permanently rid you of being a bad person in favor of being a good one. Meanwhile, Star Wars is almost totally black-and-white with its moral compass.† Luke Skywalker turns away from the

---

* I do like the idea that we should all love bad novels and bad movies because they more accurately reflect the human experience than good ones, but I worry I already live in that world a little bit and don't want to make it worse.

† We excuse Luke Skywalker for the mass murder of everyone who lives on the Death Star, for example.

Dark Side of the Force by sheer strength of will, but in real life, leaving our negative tendencies behind isn't that easy. Who's to say the day after *Return of the Jedi*, Luke didn't fall off the Dark Side wagon right away?*

Star Trek and Star Wars view personal failings differently, and though both are broad and metaphorical, they're starkly opposed in the way they depict forgiveness. In Star Wars, you have to be forgiven by other people. Darth Vader is redeemed because Luke forgives him. Han stops acting like a clown because Leia forgives him for it. The audience constantly forgives C-3PO. You get it. But that's not how Star Trek deals with personal responsibility at all. Instead, in Star Trek, the asshole side of everyone (the Dark Side) is encouraged and acknowledged as an active part of everyone's regular life, meaning Star Trek is constantly talking about what a jerk everyone is and how that's actually normal. Personal guilt is so central to all of Star Trek that *Star Trek: Voyager* constantly depicted its primary protagonist—Captain Kathryn Janeway—grappling with her own personal guilt over accidentally stranding her ship on the wrong side of the galaxy. Nearly every week, with a cup of black coffee in her hand, Janeway would lecture someone on an unethical ploy to get the starship *Voyager* back home faster, and then as soon as that person left her office, she'd turn around

---

* In the 1991 Star Wars comic book series *Dark Empire*, that is exactly what happens. Luke's relationship with the Dark Side is treated way more like a drug addiction and the moody art by Cam Kennedy reinforces this perfectly. If we see the Dark Side as "addiction," it's too bad *Trainspotting*'s Ewan McGregor had to play a goodie-Obi-Wan-Shoes in the *Star Wars* prequels. After playing Renton, he would have actually made a killer Anakin Skywalker.

and stare into space (people do this literally in Star Trek), letting us know she, too, is constantly right on the edge of breaking all the damn rules.

◆

James T. Kirk has been a dangerous figure in my life for precisely all the moral relativism Star Trek accidentally exposes. Unlike Luke Skywalker, Kirk isn't really a hero who thinks too much about what kind of person he is, but instead a person who focuses on what he can get away with. Kirk is an interesting leader, but he's no role model, and I'll never be able to shake the fact that he reminds me of my father. In Chuck Klosterman's famous Star Wars essay "Sulking with Lisa Loeb on the Ice Planet Hoth," he points out that so many people connect with Star Wars because we're all afraid of or hate our fathers. Debating this would be pointless because it's so totally accurate that it's not even funny. And yet, I think people's fathers are Darth Vader on some days and Captain Kirk on others.

When my father died in 2012 of advanced liver cirrhosis caused by drinking way too much, I reacted like a lot of people would: I drank too much. And almost six months later, I found myself staring at an empty bottle of wine I'd consumed by myself alone in my room. It was just like when Luke sees Darth Vader's severed robotic hand and then looks down at his own: we're the same kind of asshole! Children inherit the flaws or the potential flaws of their parents like fucking gangbusters, and popular science fiction either makes this fact way better or way worse. Luke is able to kick the Dark Side of the Force habit because he's a great guy, but sometimes being a great guy isn't enough to make you into the person you want to be. Plus, just forgiving Darth Vader doesn't make what Darth Vader did okay, and had Luke been able to keep him alive, you can bet everyone would want to put Vader on trial for terrible war crimes. I have issues with my dad, and maybe you do, too, but most dads aren't war criminals.

However, many dads are like Captain Kirk.* People who are in control of a seemingly pointless enterprise, who were once the boss of you, and who have occasionally unforgivable mood swings. In the 1966 episode "The Enemy Within," *Star Trek* presents perhaps what is my favorite meditation on humanity, when Captain Kirk is split into two people: his good half and his evil half. Initially, this is viewed as pretty cut-and-dried; Kirk's evil half must be stopped at all costs! He's going around drinking too much and acting like a complete barbarian. This is a version of Kirk without any boundaries, one without self-control, who's totally aggressive, dangerous, and cruel. And yet, the "good" side of Kirk slowly becomes a complete loser in this episode. Good Kirk is ineffective at making decisions and looks like he's going to cry at the drop of a hat. Say what you will about William Shatner and his overacting, but this episode of *Star Trek* alone shows he's capable of at least some kind of range. With Good Kirk a weakling and Bad Kirk a menace, the only solution to this problem is for the good side to acknowledge the bad side and for them to literally hug it out until they're

---

* Star Trek had one real dad, Captain Sisko in *Deep Space Nine*. Sisko is such a good person and a good dad that I'll not disparage him here. You can read more about him in my "Back to the Future" essay, too ("All You McFlys").

one person again. James Kirk essentially realizes that without all of his bad tendencies, the tendencies he controls, he wouldn't be the person he is. The omnipresent potential for total self-destruction is partially why he's such an effective, confident, and successful person. Kirk isn't cool in spite of his negative side, but because of it. If you hate your parents because they fucked up their lives, this, to me, is the same thing. I'll never be able to forgive my father completely in the saintly way Luke Skywalker forgives his, but I am willing to acknowledge that the part of my dad that lives inside of me is a little bit like "evil Kirk."

This is an idea *Star Trek* goes hog wild with throughout its entire original 1960s run. In "A Taste of Armageddon," the *Enterprise* rolls up on a planet that has seemingly eliminated war, only to find that the society there simulates war with computers, but still demands that "casualties" report to incineration booths every so often. Furious with this bullshit, Captain Kirk runs around the planet proclaiming what a "barbarian" he is and blows up incineration booths left and right to prove the point that actual violence is why war should be avoided, and that factoring war into a natural equation is essentially inhuman. The big Shatner speech in this one is all about realizing that maybe we are all "killers," but maybe "the instinct can be fought." Every day we can wake up and decide not to be an asshole. Sometimes we'll succeed and sometimes we'll fail, but *Star Trek* posits that it's in this struggle where our humanity is the most real.

I think my dad dug this. At least he did when I was a little kid, though he clearly forgot as he grew older. In *Return of the*

Jedi, Darth Vader tells Luke that "it's too late for me," which is probably the saddest thing in all of Star Wars. It's easy to think of Star Wars as a family tragedy and Star Trek as a positive political infomercial, but it's more nuanced than that. The going argument is that Star Trek is a hopeful vision of the future because of the peaceful nature of the Federation and the equality and equity it depicts among people (and aliens!) of various ethnicities and backgrounds. But Star Trek is also the most hopeful science fiction thing ever because it asserts that you can win the internal struggle of being your own worst enemy— that it's never too late for anyone. Which is why there are no fallen angels like Darth Vader in Star Trek and people are forced to forgive themselves, not one other.

◆

Whenever *The Wrath of Khan* was on television in my house (all the time), my father would crank up the volume on the sound system to unreasonable levels. He would futz with the bass and treble endlessly until the walls would rattle and creak like the trash compactor on the Death Star. Dads have a weird thing they do with sound systems. It's as though making another human being also requires you to pretend like you know anything about speakers. Anyway, my dad would specifically love to crank everything up during the big finale of *The Wrath*, right when Khan is delivering the Ahab speech. Naturally, for years, I never knew this speech was borrowed from Ahab, but knew it had some kind of importance. And somehow, I knew it was a quote out of context. What I didn't know then was that my father didn't know where the quote came from either.

A few years after I moved to New York, I was home in Arizona visiting my family over the holidays and somebody mentioned the idea of watching *The Wrath* on Christmas. During the climactic battle, as Spock rushes to jump-start the engines of the *Enterprise* and Khan waxes Melville, I said, "You know, I just reread *Moby-Dick*."

"What?" my father said.

"*Moby-Dick*," I said. "Khan is quoting from the ending scenes in *Moby-Dick*."

"It's Shakespeare," my dad said, sipping from his eggnog.

"Dad," I said, "it really isn't."

"Whatever," my dad said. "You were only a baby when this movie came out. I think I know what it's about."

My mom and my sister excused themselves to bed early, and my father jacked up the volume a few more notches. It was dark and almost Christmas and there wasn't any snow outside because there's never any snow in that part of Arizona. I thought about all the snow that shows up in the desert in *Star Trek III: The Search for Spock* and how Spock comes back to life first as a child and then as a teenager, and then as Leonard Nimoy. People didn't expect Spock to die in *The Wrath*, but they also didn't expect Khan to quote Melville or for the movie to end with *A Tale of Two Cities*. They remember Spock dying, though. And a few people remember him coming back in the next movie.

Everyone always forgets that Kirk has a son in *The Wrath*,

too. And though the death of Spock is talked about a lot for obvious reasons, we tend to brush aside the fact that Kirk's son is killed in *The Search for Spock*. For Star Trek to go back to being Star Trek, Captain Kirk, it seems, had to stop being someone's father. If Kirk was David's father, then he stopped being everyone's father. In *Star Trek V: The Final Frontier*, written and directed by William Shatner, Kirk and Bones joke that "other people have families," pretending that the story of their lives is more important than the people they are related to, which, if we're being honest, is exactly how a lot of people view their lives.

When the J. J. Abrams *Star Trek* movie started being promoted in 2009, one of the taglines in the trailers was "Not Your Father's Star Trek!" which is hilarious. Before my father died, he saw and LOVED Chris Pine's iteration of Captain Kirk. Pine's Kirk was handsome, funny, and a total douche bag. This, I think, was my father's idea of what I could have grown up to be: a kind of mash-up of his generation and my generation. I'm only speculating, but there are a lot of overt father issues in both the J. J. Abrams Star Treks, which is maybe why daughters and fathers as well as sons and fathers bond over them. But maybe I'm wrong and my dad liked Chris Pine's Kirk for another, easier reason. Maybe it gave him hope.

Because, after quoting Dickens, do you know the very last thing Kirk says in *The Wrath of Khan*?

I do. It's *"I feel young."*

Hipster Robots Will Save Us All

t's 2008. I'm twenty-seven years old and standing on a roof in Bushwick, Brooklyn, wearing my favorite vintage elbow-patched blazer on top and nothing but my boxer shorts on bottom. I'm attending an "underwear" party, where in addition to a cover charge of five bucks, you're also supposed to take off your pants. If you've seen any episodes of the TV show *Girls* where there's a loft party with lots of drugs, I want you to imagine that, only dirtier.

A cool nighttime summer breeze goes through my legs as I'm led—hopping—to the roof's edge. I say hopping because my feet are duct-taped together, creating a sort of upright caterpillar situation that is made all the more difficult because my arms are also duct-taped across my chest mummy-in-a-sarcophagus style. There is duct tape over my mouth, too. I'm being led by two women who are wearing cobbled-together dominatrix outfits, which aren't the porno-quality dominatrix outfits you'd see in the window of one of those sex shops, but more like what dominatrices would throw together in a postapocalyptic *Mad Max* world or perhaps in omitted chapters of Cormac McCarthy's *The Road*. We've all just met on the roof and have done a bunch of drugs and they casually ask me if they could tie me up. I say what anyone says when they are twenty-seven and attending an underwear party on a rooftop in Brooklyn and someone asks if they can tie you up. I say, of course you can tie me up. Sounds like fun.

Mr. Spock once noted that "having is not such a pleasing thing as wanting," and if you apply that to fake dominatrices coked out of their minds who are toying with your life, you start to wonder why you should ever be allowed to make any of your own decisions at all. But as the doms bring me to the edge of the building and whisper in my ear, "We could kill you, you little bitch, just drop you off this roof," the thought that goes through my mind is not *oh God, please, I want to live.* But instead: *Oh hell yeah. This is going to make a great story for my blog.* I'm twenty-seven and totally clueless, and in looking across at the distant Manhattan skyline, I'm also absurdly considering that I probably won't die anyway because I'll just wake up in a new robot body like the Cylons from *Battlestar Galactica*. If I die and my consciousness gets downloaded into an exact robot duplicate, will I be depressed or will it be awesome?

◆

Unlike the clunky robots of antiquity, the contemporary *Battlestar Galactica* Cylons are interested in looking less like robots and more like human beings,* complete with simulated flesh and blood. In the reality of *BSG*, the Cylons began their evolutionary existence as shambling, shiny robots reminiscent of walking toasters but "evolved" into more faux-organic human-looking forms. (The slurs the show uses to differentiate these kinds of Cylons are "toasters" for the robot-robots and "skin jobs" for the human-esque ones.)† In a sense, an advanced robot wanting to become human is a slightly inefficient move, like trading in a fuel-efficient vehicle for a gas-guzzler. This fact is outlined by the Cylon character Cavill (played fantastically by Dean Stockwell), who rants about his faux-human body to one of his creators in the fourth season: "I don't want to be HUMAN!" he screams. "I want to *see* gamma rays, I want to *hear* x-rays, I want to *smell* dark matter! Do you see the absurdity of what I am?" His artificial intelligence is inherently limited by his humanoid structures, which royally pisses him off because he'd rather be a more roboty robot. In Terry Bisson's short story "They're Made out of Meat," superintelligent machines discuss the grossness of life on Earth, seeing us as no more than "talking meat." These are the attitudes of robots who can easily become killer robots, the kind who, if

---

* The original *Battlestar Galactica* was a 1978–79 TV show created by Glen A. Larson, who also wrote and created *Knight Rider* and *Magnum P.I.* That version of *BSG* was the target of a frivolous lawsuit from 20th Century Fox that tried to prove the show was a rip-off of *Star Wars*. The Cylons in the old show were classic robot-robots with roboty voices and super-slow gaits.

† Late in the *BSG* game, it was revealed that several generational cycles of Cylons fighting humans had existed in the distant past. This made the singularity-style "leap" moment from the "Centurions" (the boxy, robot-style Cylons) to the human "skin jobs" really hard to pinpoint.

they do happen to be in humanoid form, are only this way because they have to be. The robots in the Terminator movies are like this: if left to their own devices, maybe they'd just be pools of liquid metal, but when the terminating needs to be done, they'll get it together to look like they've got arms and legs. In his essay "Robots," Chuck Klosterman says that if humans lose a war against robots we really have no excuse because he "can't imagine any war we've spent more time worrying about." This is the mode of thinking most popular in speculating about robots: the idea that they will rise up and destroy us. But it doesn't have to be this way if we think about robots a little harder.

Most people have fucked-up ideas about Isaac Asimov's original collection of robot stories *I, Robot*, partially because the Will Smith movie of the same name sends an opposite thematic message to the one Asimov was going for in his book. Just days before the release of *I, Robot* in the theatres in 2004, I happened to see science fiction legend and longtime Asimov friend Harlan Ellison speak at a community college in Arizona.* He begged me to skip seeing *I, Robot* for the sake of Isaac's memory, but because I *had to know*, I saw it anyway. Other than the car chases reminding me I needed to change the break-pads on my pickup truck, the movie was fairly thin. It was a by-the-numbers robots-are-going-to-kill-you movie in which Dr. Susan Calvin was changed from being a smart older scientist into some kind of dumb sexpot companion of Will Smith. The Will Smith char-

---

* Harlan Ellison wrote a screenplay for *I, Robot* that was never filmed. It's awesome.

acter, a cop investigating a robot murder, is a fabrication and not present in the book version of *I, Robot* at all.* The point is, before *I, Robot* came out most people had the idea that the book was about robots rising up to kill us, and after the movie came out, their ideas were totally reinforced. And with very few exceptions,† most big sci-fi TV shows and films have a default setting when it comes to robots. Watch out for the killer bots!

However, Asimov's impetus in writing his robot stories *at all* was that he was sick to death of sci-fi stories about killer robots *way back* in the 1930s. Check him out in his essay "The Perfect Machine":‡

> The science fiction writers could not rid themselves of the notion that the manufacture of a robot involved forbidden knowledge, a wicked aspiration on the part of a man to the abilities reserved for God. The attempt to create artificial life was an example of hubris and demanded punishment. In story after story, with grim inevitability, the robot destroyed its creator before being itself destroyed . . . [and] it was not until 1939 that, for the first time as far as I know, a science fiction writer approached the robots from a systematic engineering standpoint. Without further coyness, I will state that science fiction writer is myself.

---

* In fairness, Asimov did have some sci-fi cops in other stories and novels. Just not in *I, Robot*.

† The 2015 film *Ex Machina*. It's also split the difference: the robots are great and do kill us, but really, we had it coming. In *Ex Machina*, most of the action isn't about robot murder but instead involves questions of how to prove self-awareness. For this reason, I don't count it as a "killer robot movie."

‡ As excerpted in *Opus 100* by Isaac Asimov, Dell Publishing, New York, 1969.

Nineteen thirty-nine! Seventy-six years ago, Dr. Asimov was hell-bent on starting an intelligent revolution in science fiction, one in which the robot story would no longer be a Frankenstein's monster story. Wow. How's that one going, Dr. Asimov? Because despite writing excellent books about robots and their various machinations, the killer-robot-how-dare-we-play-God thing is still what most people think a robot story is all about.

The robots in Asimov stories aren't without conflict; it's just that the conflicts don't deal with the end of the world. My favorite story in *I, Robot* is hands down "Liar!" in which a randomly telepathic robot struggles with his programming. Based on the "laws of robotics" this robot (named Herbie) cannot allow a human being to come to harm. Herbie internalizes "harm" to mean emotional harm, and in order to make everyone feel better, he starts lying to them like crazy. You're going to get that job! That person does love you! It's not only a hysterical short story, but a heartbreaking one, too. And it proves you don't need killer robots to have conflict in your robot story.

But if we put authors' intent of various robot tales aside (as the filmmakers of *I, Robot* did), what is the net philosophical value of robots in mass culture? Everyone is not really as technophobic as science fiction movies and television would have you believe, because if they were, they certainly wouldn't be as comfortable talking to their smartphones. If looked at through the humanist lens of Asimov, the worst robot movie is *The Terminator* and the best is that oh-so-twee artificial intelligence 2013 romance *Her*. This isn't to say that the Terminator movies are bad (at least not the first two) but, more specifically, that the malevolent AI Skynet presents the conventional way movies always portray robots—they're gonna take over. True, there is emotional subtlety between Sarah Connor and the Terminator in *Judgment Day*, but I'd argue this good stuff is working from a narrative deficit of Frankenstein's monster ontology. To put it another way: the Terminator films are mildly subversive of their own genre.

If you think *Her* was a hipster movie, that's correct, because robot stories are probably better when they're meditations on grabs for spiritual authenticity rather than when they're about murder.* Despite what killer-robot stories might have you believe, the reality is that robots should and do represent something else in the culture other than a cautionary tale. What is a robot story then? Or at least, what could it be? Easy: it's a receptacle for our constant discussion about what is and is not "vintage."

◆

I told you I was wearing a *vintage* blazer on that rooftop because I was then (and maybe still am) a hipster. Like the Cylons getting called "toasters" or "skin jobs" the word "hipster" is a slur, but it's the kind you can only pick up from reading the Internet or *New York* magazine. None of the Cylons liked to self-identify as a "toaster," and I'm not crazy about self-identifying as a hipster either. But if we can agree

* I've just seen Neill Blomkamp's new robot flick *CHAPPiE*. It got killed critically, but is not a terrible robot story. If anything, it's more of an Oliver Twist homage than a hard-core robot flick. True, there are murder and violence in this movie, but the titular robot is mostly good. It's a tiny bit of progress and I think Blomkamp's heart was in the right place.

that hipsters are people who have an interest in *something* that existed before their own experience—that is, "vintage stuff"—and incorporate that vintage stuff into their day-to-day lives in an act of stylistic affectation and intentional appropriation, then yes, I am a hipster by the simple fact that I wear Chuck Taylors and, occasionally, vintage blazers. I even briefly flirted with getting into vintage vinyl records at some point, too.

The image of a hipster getting into vinyl records is where the Cylons/robots of *Battlestar Galactica* thematically live. A sufficiently evolved artificial intelligence won't have any kind of real experience with an organic body the same way I have no real experience in buying vinyl records. When I was a teenager, I nearly broke my parents' turntable trying to listen to their 1968 copy of *The White Album* while they were gone one day. I had no idea how to run it! Lieutenant Commander Data, from *Star Trek: The Next Generation*, went through this same thing, a desire to get into vintage human stuff, throughout his entire character arc on the show. In *Star Trek: First Contact*, he's even given the "gift" of "real" flesh from the evil Borg Queen, a sensation that is overwhelming to him, the same way it would be impossible for us to process "seeing" on the spectrum a new color we're not used to dealing with. Data's desire to be human is a weird affectation brought on by a love for something vintage that he doesn't understand in the same way as the people who experienced it "first." What's disturbing about Data is the fact that everyone else on the *Enterprise* encourages Data in his efforts to become "more human," when, in reality, there's nothing really wrong with him just accepting himself the way he is. Though Picard and his crew consistently stick up for Data's civil rights, they seem to reveal their own brand of robot bigotry by encouraging this desire to get into vintage human stuff as the "right way." If you've ever lived with more than one person who refuses to listen to records on anything other than records, then you know what I'm talking about.

Still, there's something endlessly pervasive about a killer-robot story, even when you've got a friendly, enlightened robot in your midst. By *Star Trek: The Next Generation*'s sixth season, the writers couldn't help but introduce a story line ("Descent Part 1") in which Data gains the power of "emotion" and turns into a complete prick. I suppose that this is, in a way, the inverse of a bad-robot story because Data turns "evil" by becoming closer to his humanity, not by becoming more "robotic." The only thing that seems to break Data out of this situation is his apparent loyalty to his crew members, because whether or not robots have emotions, robots tend to only be reflections of the hopes and dreams we pour into them.

In Star Trek, the Technological Singularity—that theoretical moment when artificial intelligence will finally lap the human mind—never occurs, because if it did, Star Trek isn't sophisticated enough to avoid turning that moment into a killer-robot story. Ray Kurzweil, author and predictor of the Technological Singularity, has asserted that in the future "machines will appear to have their own free will" and even "spiritual experiences." Taking a cue from Isaac Asimov, he also seems to believe intelligent machines will have ethics similar to their programmers or creators. If this is true, and we were to project Kurzweil's "Law of Accelerating Returns" forward into a future of super-evolved, super-bored robots,* it seems that one of the machines' "spiritual experiences" would probably include the idea of "going native," by occasionally slumming it in real or simulacrum organic bodies. These days, I can buy fake-vintage records of the Beatles, the Smiths, and the *Ghostbusters II* soundtrack at Urban Outfitters, so, you know, anything is possible.

◆

Obviously, the dominatrices don't murder me because everyone is way too hipster for that. Instead, they just lead me away from the edge of the roof, push me onto my back, duct-tape me to the roof, and ditch me. My friends and the party's host find me a few hours later. Falling asleep and being awoken by ducttape being ripped off your mouth is totally what I imagine it's like to wake up in a new robot body. In *I, Robot*, the laws of robotics state that a robot can't through *inaction* allow a human being to come to harm, which is not at all a rule when you're going to a drunken underwear party. This is also true, because you can't actually trust human beings the same way you could *potentially* trust robots. In last year's epically divisive Christopher Nolan film, *Interstellar*, a big deal is made of programming the robots at certain levels of "honesty," because otherwise they're just going to tell you all sorts of shit you probably don't want to hear. The flip side of this is that the robots in *Interstel-*

* The Law of Accelerating Returns is the idea that all of this advanced robot stuff will be exponential in its advancement.

lar are trustworthy, which of course makes most normal audience members confused as to why the robots aren't going to try and kill everyone. We've all seen *2001: A Space Odyssey*—often considered to be the best science fiction movie of all time—and we know HAL's singularity moment doesn't turn out well for anyone other than those of us in the audience. Obviously, if you're going to a drunken underwear party and you have your choice of robot friends to come with you, you'd pick Data or TARS from *Interstellar* over HAL any day of the week.

The final story of *I, Robot* is called "The Evitable Conflict," which (spoiler alert) reveals that the world is totally run by robots and very few people are actually aware of it. Of course, in a film or television show, it would be impossible to depict this kind of thing without it seeming sinister, and even in the pages of this story, Asimov gives voice to the viewpoint of robot fear. Here's a snippet from the very end of the story:

> "How horrible!"
> "Perhaps how wonderful! Think, that for all time, all conflicts are finally evitable. Only the Machines from now on, are inevitable!"

The short story "The Evitable Conflict" was published in 1950, way before Kurzweil dreamed up "the Singularity" or the Beatles even recorded albums that could be considered "vintage" by an aging hipster like me. Asimov saw robots as solving the problems of the world and being better than us. They were, to him, the next generation of friends and companions, the kind of people who, thanks to good programming, probably wouldn't let you get almost pushed off a roof at a party. If Asimov's robots ran the world, parties would be just as fun and ten times as safe. It might not make for the best science fiction movie starring Arnold or Keanu, but if the singularity does arrive in our lifetime, we might want to start making different kinds of movies about robots. There's every reason to believe they're going to dig us anyway. Because in the eyes of the right kinds of robots, we're going to be the original hipsters.

Nobody Gets Mad About Hamlet Remakes:
Rise of the Relevant Superheroes

If you ask most comic book fans the reason why Batman is so great, most will tell you it's because he's a psychologically complex person inhabiting a story laden with dark themes punctuated with lots of punching. And while Batman/Bruce Wayne may be a complex person, he's not remotely hard to comprehend, at least thematically. Batman and his enemies aren't arch or ironic insofar as everything they say reflects exactly what they do. When Christian Bale's Batman growls about being the "hero Gotham deserves," he's not kidding. A mumble-mouthed Bane says he's "Gotham's reckoning," and we believe him because he totally starts blowing up stuff right afterward. Chris Pratt's Star-Lord may have made a giant joke about being an unlikely hero, but there's still something pretty on the nose when he says, "We're the Guardians of the Galaxy, bitch" in a movie called *Guardians of the Galaxy*. After all, no one in a Lars von Trier film says, "Whoa, that's so Melancholia!"

People within comic book circles endlessly debate various qualitative elements of comic book movies: Christopher Nolan's *The Dark Knight Rises* isn't nearly as subtle or "artsy" as Tim Burton's *Batman*. Or Chris Evans was terrible in the *Fantastic Four* movies, but excellent as Captain America. But when put up against subtle dramas like *Inside Llewyn Davis*,* all comic book movies become fairly similar. *Fantastic Four: Rise of the Silver Surfer* has more in common in its DNA with *Captain America: The Winter Soldier* than either do with *In the Bedroom*. One might be a good comic book movie (*The Winter Soldier*) and one might be an embarrassing disaster perhaps best unseen by human eyes (*Silver Surfer*) but both are essentially in the same phylum. This is because it's not like there's an *X-Men* movie filmed in black-and-white directed by Alexander Payne that is just about an elderly version of Professor X living in an old-folks home using his psychic powers to rig bingo night.

A lot of contemporary comic book movies like *Man of Steel* or *X-Men: First Class* might tend to begin like "regular" movies,† but they seldom stay that way. And beyond the fact that comic book heroes are originally "for children," one of the reasons mainstream critics tend to deride (or at least hold a bias against) this stuff is probably because comic book movies assert an

---

* Does the presence of two actors from *Inside Llewyn Davis* (Oscar Isaac and Adam Driver) in the new Star Wars movie mean it will be the most arty/nuanced Star Wars yet? Let's meet at the bar in 2016 and talk about it. First round is on me.

† The opposite of this would be the Joel Schumacher Batman movies: *Batman Forever* and *Batman and Robin*, both of which start like comic book movies and end like an acid-filled, hallucinogenic rave with neon glow-sticks everywhere.

apparent lack of artistic subtly. A. O. Scott of the *New York Times* complained that *The Avengers* demanded "obedience" from the audience to absorb the film's pop narrative while also permanently suspending viewers' disbelief. And yet, serious connoisseurs of the arts wouldn't bat an eye at the overtly on-the-nose nature of opera or even of mainstream musicals. If musicals and operas live in an alternate dimension where it's perfectly natural for characters to burst into song to express their feelings in a direct and obvious way, why are costumed heroes given the critical shaft?

Part of the answer is because the times are a-changin' and we're just now, as a culture, getting used to superheroes. Twenty years from now, assuming they are still around, DC Comics will turn one hundred and Marvel will be about ninety. Thinking about that in reverse: I've never lived in a world without superhero movies. People of the generation right after me have never lived in a world without *good* superhero movies. If this keeps happening, by the time I'm fifty years old, superheroes will likely be a cultural institution on par with Shakespeare, opera, musicals, and anything else that everyone just accepts as "normal." But people who are twenty to thirty years *older* than me might associate superheroes with the nana-nana-nana-nana BIFF/POW/ZOWIE/ZAP aesthetic. And some of these folks are still really successful (and good, I might add) critics. It may sound a bit morbid, but when those people stop writing movie reviews all of this will change.*

---

* Similarly, future cultural critics who are like five years old right now will read this essay of mine in their thirties and find my assertions totally

Here's where I need to address a common complaint among mainstream critics and geeks alike: superheroes are rebooted or remade too quickly. In 2016, just four years after Christian Bale completed his trilogy as Batman, Ben Affleck is set to make his debut as the caped crusader in *Batman v. Superman: Dawn of Justice.* When the casting of Affleck was announced in 2013, a good portion of the world's population freaked out either in support or in opposition. At the 2014 New York Comic Con, I personally saw at least three dudes wearing T-shirts emblazoned with Ben Affleck's name on a Batman logo with a giant *X* over it, indicating they were anti-Batffleck. Sadly, this brand of alarmism is nothing new. Tons of fans wrote letters to Warner Bros. in the '80s because they were furious that "Mr. Mom," Michael Keaton, was allowed to play Batman. We're all susceptible to this and even I was irked when Andrew Garfield—whom I viewed as a guy who was on *Doctor Who* one time—was cast as Spider-Man. But, the thing is, there's no reason to get mad or worried about any of this because the characters themselves are entering into the zeitgeist in exactly the same way literary or mythological figures did in the good old days. Were you offended when Liam Neeson was cast as Zeus in *Clash of the Titans?* Probably not. Remember when Leo DiCaprio and Carey Mulligan were cast in *The Great Gatsby?** Who was mad about that? No one. Because there's been a

---

quaint. They'll also probably have absorbed the essay through some sort of futuristic reading cream, but whatever.

   * Carey Mulligan also starred in the same season of *Doctor Who* as Andrew Garfield, in 2007. Then they did *Never Let Me Go* together. Why are neither in the new Star Wars? It's baffling.

cinematic Jay Gatsby before and there will be one again. Batman, Spider-Man, Superman, and, shockingly, Ant-Man, will likely be around just as long as "classic" canonical characters. If you're irritated they remade Spider-Man too fast or you're worried they're rebooting Batman too quickly after *The Dark Knight Rises*, just wait until they remake all of this stuff for the fortieth time in the twenty-second century. You'll be so mad!

A 2012 article in the *Los Angeles Times* is a great example of what seems to me to be a misunderstanding or less-than-thoughtful explanation of the remake/reboot phenomenon. In the piece, Neal Gabler rails against the young generation of millennials who "don't think of movies as art the way so many boomers did." Now despite Gabler making a problematic us-versus-them argument, I don't think there's any compelling evidence to suggest the appreciation of film as art has anything to do with the reboot phenomenon, nor being young. Being ignorant and unappreciative of great stories knows no generational boundaries. Gabler's analysis—which represents a larger knee-jerk argument that you hear all the time—seems to suggest that remakes (or *restagings* if you will) of beloved stories and characters are somehow an epidemic brought on by an ignorant generation's lack of understanding about the artistic merit of films, and therefore a new phenomenon. But remakes are nothing new. For centuries around the globe, there have been countless remakes of plays by Shakespeare that probably didn't look a lot like they would have looked in the Globe. And sure, scholars of Shakespeare still freak out about various interpretations, updating, omissions, abridgments, and so forth, but for most of us, *Hamlet* is a story that we will see at some point in our lives and be all the better for it. Did Steve Martin's *Roxanne* harm the essence of *Cyrano de Bergerac*? No. I love all versions of *Cyrano*. And I like both the Tobey Maguire Spider-Man AND the Andrew Garfield Spider-Man. Now I'm learning we may get yet another new Spider-Man in 2017. Bring it on! The Gérard Depardieu version of *Cyrano* may be the definitive one, but it doesn't mean the José Ferrer version sucks. Christopher Nolan's *Dark Knight* trilogy is now considered along the same definitive lines as the Gérard Depardieu version of *Cyrano*, but it doesn't mean Ben Affleck's new Batman will somehow ruin that or make Michael Keaton irrelevant.

Most children who are familiar with fairy tales rarely read the original text of the Grimm brothers or Hans Christian Andersen first. And while this might be a shame, it doesn't mean anything has necessarily been ruined, nor does it indicate a lack of appreciation for the stories. A good number of people who saw the *Avengers* movie did understand these characters from their comic book roots. Another, larger portion of the population didn't read comics before or after. Should we care? Is this that big of a deal? As we've established, comic book source material that is *commonly* adapted into film is relatively unsubtle and over-the-top. And at the risk of getting stoned to death by comic book purists, I'll ask, is it possible that these iterations of big, broad characters and themes work *better* as films?

Because the films constituting the Marvel Cinematic Universe can be technically conceived on the convincing scope that they're made on, doesn't that mean these stories and characters are reaching more people than they would if the characters were limited to comic books? If you equate the success of the Marvel movies with Shakespeare passing into the public domain, what I'm saying should start to make sense. Nobody who puts on a serious production of a Shakespeare play thinks *oh, ours will just be okay.* They want to do the source material justice. And that's what's happening every time our culture remakes a superhero. If Shakespeare were around now, he'd probably be writing plays *about* superheroes.

The idea that the movie isn't as good as the source material because it contradicts the author's vision is another criticism of comic book movies. We might claim Batman was "created" by Bob Kane, but most people will tell you he was co-created by Bill Finger. So, are we seeing a vision of Batman that is true to Kane's or Finger's original conception of him when we go to see the latest Batman movie? Absolutely not. From Alan Moore to Frank Miller to Jeph Loeb to Gail Simone to Marguerite Bennett to artists like Neal Adams, Alex Ross, Jim Lee, Tim Sale, Lee Bermejo, Becky Cloonan, and countless more, the image and words of Batman aren't the purview of any one sacred person. And this is true for every single other superhero, too. There are certainly controversies over who gets original credit—Stan Lee versus Jack Kirby, and Bob Kane versus Bill Finger are notable ones—but my larger point doesn't have much to do with that. Debating whether or not Shakespeare was real or actually one hundred million monkeys doesn't make *Much Ado About Nothing* stop existing. And the same is true—or perhaps *truer*—with comic book heroes. Comics have *always* had several different narrative voices behind the scenes, which means that by the time the stories get translated into big, watchable movies, all of those narrative voices are condensed down into a single composite story. Because there's probably a lot of good stuff left over, who wouldn't want to make another movie?

More interestingly, the fact that comic books do have a composite narrative means they're more accessible to a larger group of people than any other type of narrative fiction, ever. Most people don't think Batman = Bob Kane or Batman = Christopher Nolan. Most people think Batman = ME. The public thinks it owns Batman, which is how mythology works. Who is the author of the Greek myths? It's not exactly Homer. Because we are the ones who have kept the myths alive over centuries by retelling the stories in a myriad of different forms.

So what else might bother someone about the reboot phenomenon, other than misplaced dislike of millennials or superhero bigotry? Probably money. If you hate superhero movies because you see them as cynical money grabs from the studio, I can understand where you're coming from, but would implore you to think about that critique a little bit harder. Just because something is a moneymaker does not automatically make it "trash," and just because something is "trash" doesn't mean it's not culturally relevant. The very first issue of *Captain America* was sold in 1940 and featured Cap punching out Hitler.* This was a political statement because it was a full year before the United States entered World War II. It was also a great idea for a moneymaking comic book, too.

---

* As happens with a lot of periodicals, the comic was put on sale in advance of the publication date printed on the cover. So, the first issue of *Captain America* is the March 1941 issue, but it was sold in December 1940.

The current superhero boom is the future of human storytelling unfolding in front of us, but because we're at the beginning of something new, it's hard to see the overall anthropological impact. I can't convince you of the long mythological tradition of superheroes as effectively as Grant Morrison can in his book *SuperGods* or the way Margaret Atwood opines in her book *In Other Worlds*, but I am urging you to try and think about the reactions you might have to superhero movies with a little more gentleness and with eyes toward the future rather than the present or past. Have you ever read the reviews of *A Christmas Carol*? A few were similar to articles I've read about *The Avengers*. What about *Moby-Dick*? It was about as well liked as *Spider-Man 2*. We're not going backward, nor are we out of ideas. For a culture that tells stories, superheroes don't represent stagnation, nor anything to get alarmed about. Instead, like the superpowered people themselves, we're entering a new evolutionary stage of narrative development. And we're doing it in a way we've always done: by telling our favorite stories over and over and over again.

The Fans Awaken

Everyone tells you that the best way to be nice to yourself and have a fulfilling life is to never have regrets, or if you do, to never focus on them. This advice is fine, but it also exclusively applies to you thinking about yourself when you are by yourself. A regret is a thing you think might have been a mistake, but a mistake is a thing that other people know is a mistake. If we group both regrets and mistakes into the same phylum—let's call that phylum "hypothetical trigger moments leading to more preferable alternate universes"—then we can begin to understand why it must be so hard to live each day if you are George Lucas. Even if he doesn't think he has any regrets, there's a whole world of people who are more than willing to point out his mistakes. So, *The Force Awakens* is practically here. What kind of Star Wars fans are we going to be?

In 2006, during the early days of online personality quizzes like "Which *Sex and the City* Character Are You?" (Samantha) or "Which Spice Girls Song Is About Your Life?" ("Wannabe"),

I took another quiz over and over again, hoping to get a different result. The quiz was "What Kind of Star Wars Fan Are You?" and the answer I got was "You're a Hater!" Not only could I not post that result to my Myspace.com account with any kind of arch glee; I was also depressed by what I perceived to be an online-quiz mistrial. How could I be a hater? I loved Star Wars! Just because I *knew better* than George Lucas which way Star Wars should have gone didn't make me a hater. But it was true enough, precisely because I certainly complained about Star Wars more than I praised it. Not only was being a Star Wars/George Lucas "hater" something I often did; it was also, apparently, a real thing. And because it was something someone had thought to put as a result in a Myspace quiz, it meant being accused of being a hater was worse than just a surprise. It was common.

Super fans are all more than willing to tell George Lucas—or any other creator of sci-fi, fantasy, or comic books—that something is rotten in Denmark (or Tatooine) and that we the people won't stand for it. Sir Arthur Conan Doyle had a contentious relationship with his readers, while William Shatner has practically made a second career out of apologizing to Star Trek fans for how much he used to mock them. The playground peacekeeping philosophy most people's moms would recommend here is "live and let live." If we don't like Steven Moffat's writing on *Doctor Who* or *Sherlock*, maybe we should just throw our hands up and say, "Hey, I can't write a TV show. What do I know?" If George R. R. Martin is taking too long with the next book in *A Song of Ice and Fire*, maybe we should stop complaining and try to write our own epic fantasy novels series. And if George Lucas wants to try and ruin Star Wars over and over again, then maybe we should just be more understanding, because, after all, *we* didn't make Star Wars. Wasn't it his to ruin in the first place?

As it turns out, no.

These days, it looks like what the fans have long suspected has been proven true: Star Wars is *ours*. We don't need to live and let live with George Lucas, because, in this ever-changing galaxy, it's time to say live and let die. As of 2012, when he sold Star Wars to Disney, George Lucas was longer in charge of Star Wars! Now an entirely new group of people—specifically led by J. J. Abrams*—is poised to either save Star Wars from ruin or, more unlikely, ruin it further. As I write this, the zeitgeist is holding its breath as Star Wars readies itself to make a comeback with the release of *Star Wars Episode VII: The Force Awakens*.

Of course, in order to make a comeback, it means you need to have sucked for a while. This happens all the time with bands and musicians, except that the cultural impact of a good U2 album versus a bad U2 album is nothing compared to the mammoth relevance of Star Wars. If we looked at the most important pop events—TV, movies, music—of the twentieth century, Star Wars is certainly in the top ten. If we only talk about pop events after 1945, Star Wars is easily in the top four; I can't think of anything bigger than Star Wars beyond Michael Jackson, the Beatles, and Oprah Winfrey. I'm not saying Star

---

* For now. Rian Johnson has been tapped to direct the sequel to *The Force Awakens*. Maybe J.J. couldn't take the pressure? Maybe nobody wants to direct three Star Wars movies in a row?

Wars is better than every other pop event of the previous century; it's just that it's undeniably gargantuan in how much it means to people. If a bad U2 album is a meteor, then *Songs of Innocence* is the kind that burns up in the atmosphere. If a bad Star Wars movie is like a meteor, then *The Phantom Menace* is the kind that killed the dinosaurs. But how did Star Wars get ruined and who really did the ruining? Is George Lucas the only person with regrets?

◆

Everything could have always almost been something else. This is true of life in a *Sliding Doors* kind of way, and obviously true of everything having to do with pop culture,* specifically these geeky interests that permeate everyone's dreams and nightmares so constantly. There's an earworm of a song by the forgettable and truly terrible band Everclear,† in which one of the lines is "like a Star Wars poster on my bedroom door." Obviously, we know for a fact that Star Wars, and Star Wars posters, *did* actually indirectly create the band Everclear, because there's no alternate dimension without Star Wars that also includes Everclear. But there are all kinds of terrible crap that more directly exist because of Star Wars,‡ so don't blame it too harshly. The alternate universe blame game is both more fun and sadder than that, because even if Everclear can't exist without Star Wars, what's more telling about that line is that

* See all essays in this book for "proof."
† The song is called "Wonderful," and it's just the worst.
‡ Science fiction critics a few generations older than I am would argue the terrible crap I refer to here is "everything."

the band doesn't only sing the words "Star Wars" but rather "a Star Wars *poster*." The fandom of the thing is imbedded in everyday jargon in a way that is more important, or more revealing, than the thing itself.

Because I came of age in the '90s, let's take another popular song from that era, this time a good one. In the epic rap hit "Hypnotize," Biggie Smalls informs us of all kinds of stuff that he's up to while a chorus of other people let us know what he is capable of, specifically his ability to sometimes "hypnotize" them just with his words. One line from Biggie goes like this: "Hit 'em with the Force like Obi," which, no matter how you slice it, is a reference to Obi-Wan Kenobi. If it was just either "the Force" or "Obi" without the other word, it would be something we might be able to dismiss. But infinitely more clever than those Everclear jokers, Biggie actually insinuates the Star Wars lineage of his lyric in another way: Obi-Wan Kenobi has the ability to "hypnotize" certain people with his "words," meaning the Notorious B.I.G. is obviously some kind of Jedi Knight.

Imagining a universe without Star Wars but one that *does* include Biggie Smalls is possible, but it's also no fun. What is fun is the fact that just a small dip into totally innocuous pop art—forgettable and iconic alike—reveals a pervasive Star Wars fandom that is more omnipresent than any other collection of popular fiction I can think of. I mean, to my knowledge, there aren't any references to *Citizen Kane* or Shakespeare in any other Biggie tracks, right?

But let's head back to that Star Wars poster on the bedroom door. Every couple of months a geek blog (occasionally one I write for) will "discover" a cache of old Star Wars photos or concept art or unused promotional art, throw all of the art or photos onto the blog, and breathlessly declare what might have been. With the original *Star Wars*, there's a ton of material that predates the release of the movie partially because Lucas hired an absolutely brilliant PR guy named Charles Lippincott, who saw the potential to get the existing science fiction and fantasy fandom excited about *Star Wars* in 1976, a year prior to its release. He pushed for a Star Wars presentation at Worldcon that year, as well as at San Diego Comic Con. Ralph McQuarrie's original concept art was on display, as were costumes, and Mark Hamill was there, too! If there are any time-traveling Star Wars fans from the future hanging out at the '76 Comic Con, they're either taking a shitload of selfies with Hamill, or poised to make a fortune off of retro merchandise. In any case, if you don't think having a convention presence helped solidify *Star Wars'* box office success, ask yourself where all those people came from on opening day in 1977. Like all good hype machines, *Star Wars* was popular before anyone knew what they were so in love with.

Some of this "original" Lippincott-encouraged press material contains references to Buck Rogers and Flash Gordon.*

---

* Buck Rogers originally was conceived as Anthony Rogers in Philip Francis Nowlan's 1928 novel *Armageddon 2419 A.D.* Subsequently Buck appeared in radio shows, comic strips, and movie serials. Buster Crabbe played Buck Rogers in 1930s serials, and later played Flash Gordon. In the late '70s a TV revival of Buck Rogers starring Gil Gerard existed, which, without irony, was made possible by the popularity of Star Wars. Flash Gordon was a comic strip character who started appearing in 1934. He is connected to Buck Rogers specifically because he was created by Alex Raymond to compete with Buck Rogers.

One unused poster in particular says "First Buck Rogers, then Flash Gordon, now Luke Skywalker," evoking science fiction heroes of yore in order to get existing sci-fi fans on board with this newfangled Star Wars product. Here's the thing, though: that poster was almost a different poster altogether, one that didn't say "Luke Skywalker" at all, but instead, only "Flash Gordon." Before writing *Star Wars* itself, George Lucas literally wanted to remake Flash Gordon, but was unable to secure the legal rights, so it would seem he began work on something else, sometime around 1973. That thing had a lot of different names, but most sources seem to indicate it was called *The Journal of the Whills* and featured a guy named Mace Windy.* Countless permutations of this original outline and/or story treatment exist, but suffice it to say, it eventually became known as something called *The Star Wars* and featured a guy named Annakin Starkiller.† For many of you, this might all sound familiar. We know Annakin becomes "Anakin," Starkiller obviously evolves to "Skywalker," and in a pre–Mark Zuckerberg move, "The Star Wars" dropped its article to become "Star Wars." At this point, let's pause and pretend that we're mad about all of these changes, because we are faux purists who only believe in the original version of something before it got "ruined."

---

* Obviously, this became Samuel L. Jackson's character, Mace Windu, in the prequels.

† For many, countless permutations are nothing new. In 2013, Dark Horse Comics released a limited run called *The Star Wars*, which supposedly showed the "original" version of Lucas's idea in comic format. While really pretty and interesting, the idea that it's the "original" story is such bullshit. There are so many different versions of Lucas's original story that the word "original" starts to lose its meaning the same way the name Anakin Skywalker has no meaning next to that of his alter ego, Darth Vader.

Here's a recap of the history of Star Wars from 1973-ish to 1976-ish with my ruining goggles in place:

First, Lucas wants to remake (ruin) *Flash Gordon,* but he can't get the rights so he decides to write his own thing, which he proceeds to ruin even as he's inventing it. He titles this *The Journal of the Whills*, but changes (ruins) it to be something more commercial: *The Star Wars.* He drops the "the" from the title (ruining it) and then decides he wants to incorporate elements of classic Kurosawa films, which will surely ruin them by homage. Lucas originally wants to have the Death Star show up in a later movie, but decides to change (ruin) it and moves it into the first movie. Han Solo is supposed to be a green-skinned alien, but Lucas changes (ruins) that because it's going to be too expensive, which of course is totally pathetic. Deke (or Annakin) Starkiller is obviously a way better name than Skywalker, so Lucas decides to ruin Luke and Annakin the moment he invents both of them.

Wow, don't you wish you'd seen *The Journal of the Whills*—or better yet, George Lucas's *Flash Gordon*—before Lucas went and ruined everything?

Of course you don't.

However, most of us are correctly angry that Lucas screwed with the classic trilogy when he released the "Special Editions" in 1997 and 1998. In the interests of letting the good work countless others have done in enumerating all the changes performed on these films speak for itself, I'll just describe the special editions of the movies with three words: random laser bolts. I mean this both metaphorically and literally, but more literally.* Though to Lucas, the random laser bolt fired by Greedo in the special edition of *A New Hope* isn't random at all. Instead, it's an edit. Throughout the history of his Star Wars from *The Journal of the Whills* to *Revenge of the Sith*, George Lucas has constantly altered the information by making shit up on the fly. If you dig into research on how all three original films were written, directed, and edited in postproduction,† you'll start to suspect the finality of these stories was a little half-baked throughout the entire process. If you watch just *one* interview with Lucas where he discusses the making of any of the three prequels, you'll be sure of it.

The *Star Wars* prequel trilogy—*The Phantom Menace*, *Attack of the Clones*, and *Revenge of the Sith*—offends purist fans of the original trilogy for the exact same reason the special editions do. And that's because both smack of revisionism after the fact. In the original release of *Star Wars*, we think Han murders Greedo in cold blood, but in the special edition, Greedo "shoots first." The *meaning* of the scene was changed and so we all got super-pissed. But the prequels are the same. We thought the Force worked a certain way in the old movies, but then Liam Neeson tells us something different about little critters living in our bloodstream who talk to the Force in *The Phantom*

---

* I know there are no "literal" laser bolts because laser bolts don't exist or whatever, but just calm down. If you watch Merriam-Webster's "Ask the Editor" on YouTube like I do, you'll learn "literally" almost literally doesn't mean anything.

† This research can be found mostly in the out-of-print and amazing book *Star Wars: The Annotated Screenplays*, by Laurent Bouzereau.

Menace. Leia says she remembers her mother in *Return of the Jedi*, but then, in *Revenge of the Sith*, Natalie Portman dies before she can even coo at the just-born Leia baby. Lucas revised the origin story of Leia, but still left the original scene in the special edition of *Return of the Jedi.** If Episodes 1–6 of Star Wars were not a series of films but, instead, a single novel, that one scene with Leia—among many other maddening problems—would be a serious continuity error. Still, in his (kind of) defense, if Lucas had made *Revenge of the Sith* before he'd released the special edition of *Return of the Jedi* you can bet he would have messed with the part where Leia talks to Luke about her mother. Hell, there may have even been a digitally inserted thought bubble above Carrie Fisher's head featuring Natalie Portman crying or, even worse, brushing her hair while talking dirty to Anakin. But there isn't and he didn't because George Lucas's revision process of the entire Star Wars saga is beyond postmodern. If we extend the idea of Episodes 1–6 as composing a single novel, it would be a novel that was constantly being revised by a time-traveling author who hadn't bothered to reread the parts of the manuscript that he was

---

* Of course, there are multiple "Special Editions," with variations great and small. The initial special editions were theatrical, then made for VHS. And then, in 2004, there was a DVD release. The DVD special edition of *Return of the Jedi* was the most controversial of all because the ghost of Anakin Skywalker was no longer played by Sebastian Shaw but, instead, by Hayden Christensen. Obviously, there's no way Lucas could have put the ghost of Hayden into the 1998 special edition of *Return of the Jedi*, because Hayden would have been like seventeen years old and he and George Lucas didn't even know each other then. Still, I often wonder what would happen if Hayden's ghost were digitally inserted into a bunch of other classic movies. Think of him in the final scenes of *The Wizard of Oz*! Or better yet, *Casablanca*!

changing. If we think of Lucas as a time-traveling novelist working on a sentence level, and Episodes 1–6 were each a sentence, then the episodes would be sentences that only sort of go together. In at least one documentary about the prequels, Lucas described aspects of Star Wars as "poetry," which abstractly might be more accurate, but somehow also insulting to real poets. All of this can make you angry, but it also does prove George Lucas is a mad genius.

Still, if you think this hop-skip-and-a-jump story-revision bullshit began with the special editions and continued through the prequels, you're about as wrong as Luke was when he fantasized about having sex with his sister. We tend to forgive Lucas for revisions that take place after the fact, provided of course that those changes *work*. No one complains about the improved, cool-looking X-Wing dogfights in the special edition of *A New Hope* for the same reason nobody complains about Darth Vader being Luke Skywalker's father or Leia turning out to be Luke's sister. All that stuff works. Which doesn't change the fact that both Darth Vader being Luke's dad and Leia being Luke's sister were elements of the story that were worked out during Lucas's revision process, which, as we now understand, is a revision process that doesn't operate under the normal rules of linear time.

In the late '70s, the screenplay for *The Empire Strikes Back* was initially commissioned as a work-for-hire to be written by the excellent fantasy novelist Leigh Brackett. Though it looks like she and Lucas collaborated a substantial amount on this, there are a lot of elements of Brackett's screenplay that obviously didn't make it into the final movie, most notably a scene in which the ghost of Luke Skywalker's father is not a bad guy, but just another ghost who talks to Luke. Yoda is called "Minch"; Lando might have been a clone left over from the Clone Wars; a secret crystal hidden in Luke's lightsaber gives him a secret message; and so forth. When Leigh Brackett sadly passed away, George Lucas and his *Raiders of the Lost Ark* screenwriting buddy Lawrence Kasdan took over finishing the script for *Empire*. For those of us who are really serious about this stuff, this is the real moment when George Lucas starts to truly care about Star Wars in a way that actually creates the larger mythology. Here, he invents his wackado revision process: "Sure, Darth Vader is Luke's *father*, always has been." And what's totally brilliant about this is that, broadly speaking, his retroactive continuity worked so well that it redefined a global phenomenon that was already a global phenomenon!

The Empire Strikes Back is an aberration in film history that should almost never have happened. No matter what anyone tells you (including me), all movie sequels are just ways of getting more money out of the same thing. Even direct-to-video sequels to *Starship Troopers* weren't made out of a love for the characters or the franchise. So, when sequels are actually *good* it's a total miracle. I say "miracle" specifically, because it almost never happens.

Lucas can't take all the credit for *The Empire Strikes Back* being as good as (or, probably, better than) the original *Star Wars*. Director Irvin Kershner famously altered a lot of stuff as the cameras were rolling. When Han Solo is getting ready to be frozen in the carbonite chamber, Leia can't take it anymore and says, "I love you!" to which Han Solo jerkishly quips,

"I know." Instantly more classic than *Gone with the Wind*'s "Frankly, my dear, I don't give a damn," this line was originally written by Lucas (or Kasdan or, doubtfully, Brackett) as "I love you, too." In collaboration with Harrison Ford, Kershner changed the line on set and turned this unimaginative dialogue into a living, breathing explosion of unforgettable romance. Like many hard-core Star Wars fans who are also George Lucas haters, I used to constantly point out that Kershner (and maybe Kasdan and maybe Brackett and *maybe* producer Gary Kurtz) was the true genius of *The Empire Strikes Back*, and George Lucas was just sort of a useless man-behind-the-curtain. A non-wizard of Oz. But I was wrong.

From a certain point of view, Irvin Kershner is actually just an accomplice to George Lucas's make-it-up-as-you-go-along revision process. If anything, the total success of *The Empire Strikes Back*, thanks to Kershner's directorial skill,* proved to Lucas that he (and his cohorts) could get away with anything. They were just like the Rebels! Don't have a plan for how these movies are going to turn out? Don't worry! We'll just make it up as we go along! This kind of admirable nonsense is why *The*

---

* I've been dying to say this for years, but it seems like poor Irvin Kershner was only allowed one good sequel. He directed *RoboCop 2* and a random non-canon James Bond movie called *Never Say Never Again*. *RoboCop 2* is borderline unwatchable and *Never Say Never Again* was a James Bond movie starring Sean Connery that actually lost at the box office to a James Bond movie released the same year starring Roger Moore (*Octopussy*). How is a James Bond movie called *Octopussy* better than *Never Say Never Again*? I know. This sounds fake. But it's true! Though I'm sure if Kershner had directed *Octopussy* it would have been even better than it already is. (Which is to say, marginally. I mean, it's called "Octopussy.") He's not to blame for these bad movies he directed, but it's not like he had the magic touch with established franchises.

Empire Strikes Back is a miracle and not a masterpiece. Or to put it another way: it was a miracle the year it came out, but it's a masterpiece *now*. And ultimately, there's something totally rock and roll about George Lucas's borderline dismissal of convention in making the original *Star Wars* trilogy. Here was someone so disinterested in this wonderful thing he'd created that he actually tried to farm out the screenplay to someone else. Like Conan Doyle before him, George Lucas, at least in the early days, clearly felt like he was above the "kids movie" he'd made, and so, he treated the process by which he made the films immaturely. This isn't a dig. This is why he's awesome.

◆

Still, we're dealing with a process that seems like it shouldn't have worked. And when you get to *Return of the Jedi*, the sad truth is, it didn't. As a child my favorite movie (period) was *Return of the Jedi*. There are a lot of dumb little-kid reasons for this (the Ewoks are cute; Admiral Ackbar is a talking fish person), but I think the overwhelming real reason is that Luke Skywalker resolves all of his family's problems and that everyone lives happily ever after. If *A New Hope* was a homage to an old adventure serial like *Flash Gordon*, and *The Empire Strikes Back* was a bizarre, dark hybrid of contemporary filmmaking and Shakespearean tragedy, then *Return of the Jedi* is a good old-fashioned fairy tale. Luke Skywalker rides into town, rescues his best friend, gets his dad to kick his bad habits, and everyone sits around the campfire and tells stories about it. Throw in some speeder-bikes and a ton of awesome monsters and you've got a movie that feels more like a family film than any of the other Star Wars movies, especially the prequels. When you grow up, though, you begin to detest this movie because it feels like it took one look at all the dark and twisted themes of *The Empire Strikes Back* and said, "Never mind."

For one thing, Luke Skywalker's character seems to have developed in between *Empire* and *Jedi*. When we leave Luke in the final moments of *Empire*, he's practically just recovered from crying and almost (maybe?) attempting suicide.* From his first moments in *Jedi*, however, he's a total badass, a man who takes no shit and gives zero fucks as to what anyone thinks of him. How did he become this way? In addition to advice, did Yoda also give Luke some Prozac or lithium or Ritalin? Has all of that stuff just finally kicked in by the time of *Return of the Jedi*? We're meant to think of *Return of the Jedi* as Luke's journey toward becoming a grown-up, but the fact is, he's pretty much this person at the beginning of the movie: calm, confident, and willing to face up to consequences. True, we see Luke being "tempted" by the Dark Side of the Force when the Emperor is making fun of him for fighting with Vader. But as many have argued, the audience never really believes there's much for Luke to gain by turning to the Dark Side, meaning it's a nonchoice and doesn't play that well dramatically.† Perhaps we are

---

* When Luke lets himself drop into the abyss in Cloud City toward the end of *Empire*, I guess you could argue he knew he'd get rescued somehow because he trusted the Force—a religious leap of faith. But, it's also just as easy to interpret this as Luke defiantly killing himself rather than joining what he perceives as pure evil.

† Red Letter Media's satirical Mr. Plinkett videos make this point fairly effectively, specifically in their review of *Revenge of the Sith*, in which they assert that Anakin actually does have a reason for turning that Luke never

a little worried Luke might die, but his soul has already been saved, so as nice as it is to see him happy, it's a little boring.

Similarly, in *Return of the Jedi* after Han Solo is rescued from the vile clutches of Jabba the Hutt, there's not much tension for that character either. No longer as roguish or as funny,* Han Solo is given the rank of general and spends most of the movie playing second fiddle to Luke. In *Empire*, Luke, Han, and Leia felt more like an ensemble, as they did in the first film, only more so. But in *Jedi*, Leia and Han are mostly just there to support Luke and the basic "plot." Harrison Ford has said repeatedly in interviews that he wanted Han to get killed in *Jedi* to bring the character's arc to a more tragic conclusion. There are also indications from Kasdan that it would be a good idea for Lando to get killed by the Sarlacc toward the start of the movie to let people know that particular monster was "for real." True or not, this seems to all have been shot down by Lucas in an effort to demonstrate that the good guys were all going to win and that, just this once, everybody lives. In a sense, even people who die get to live. At the end of the film, the last thing we see are the ghosts of Obi-Wan, Yoda, and Anakin, meaning that the only people who really died in the

---

had. Part of this is just that Luke has a healthier social life—i.e., he has better friends than Anakin did, meaning he feels more secure as a person.

* It's a simple fact that any movie with Harrison Ford in which he doesn't get to say funny things isn't as good as one in which he does. This is actually the only reason you need to explain why *Indiana Jones and the Kingdom of the Crystal Skull* is so awful: Ford doesn't have any funny lines. The exception to this rule is, naturally, *Blade Runner.*

movie were either minor characters (those poor Rebel pilots) or bad guys.

Leia, sadly, has the least amount of character development other than discovering she's Luke's sister, which makes her ability to pick Han as her boyfriend a little easier. If this was truly the end of a three-part story about these three people, you'd think Leia and Han would have been able to do more soul-searching, the way they did in *Empire*. This is doubly strange because even though we learn Leia is Luke's sister (and therefore a member of the Skywalkers) she doesn't use the Force or do anything coolly reminiscent of having Jedi powers. I attempted a full rewrite of *Return of the Jedi* many times when I was in my early twenties, but for me it comes down to one thing that could have easily been changed. When Han, Chewie, and Leia are all on Endor captured by the Empire, they are saved, we discover, because the Ewoks rise up and throw some rocks on the Stormtroopers. Why did the writing go in this direction when the story has Leia sitting right there?

Imagine this instead: the Empire has everybody cornered, Han is out of ideas, Chewie is shitting his non-pants, and C-3PO, for once, is speechless. The Ewoks are obviously no match for the Empire, and as their little furry bodies are burned, Leia kneels down to surrender to the commander of the Imperial troops. But then, as she rises, she also brings her hand up, Vader-style, and Force-chokes the lead bad guy. Then, in a display of godlike power, Leia uses the Force to throw around a few Stormtroopers in midair. Han's blaster levitates back into his hand and he starts blowing away the bad guys.

"I never knew you had that in you, sweetheart," Han says.

"You know," Leia says, panting, exhausted but resolved to win, "neither did I."

There's never a real on-screen payoff dealing with Leia being Luke's sister and in the slapdash way these movies were obviously written, it seems like a massive oversight. Plus, it would have been so cool to have given *Return of the Jedi*'s title added meaning by demonstrating the dominance of Luke, the redemption of Vader, and then, ultimately, the rise of Leia. It was all right there waiting to happen. Instead, the lasting impression of Princess Leia in *Return of the Jedi* was of her in a bikini outfit from the beginning of the movie. Even Barbarella had more agency. And she was naked in her first scene.

◆

Up until the sale of Star Wars to Disney in 2012, I think, in Lucas's mind he was still revising *The Star Wars*, even after everything had been released. Despite everything that I've argued for in this essay, and throughout this book, Star Wars is "just" a movie, meaning we can't get as angry with it as we do with real people. Or, to put it another way, if we do happen to get that angry, we should at the very least *think about why*. If video killed the radio star, then Star Wars fans are what made Star Wars sacred. We took Star Wars away from George Lucas (and from all the actors, too!) and we were 100 percent successful. Saying Star Wars is a victim of its own success is an understatement on par with "The teachings of Moses are popular," or "There are decent acoustics in Carnegie Hall."

◆

In 2004, my friend Brittany had a problem. She was taking a George Lucas/Steven Spielberg film studies course and one of the assignments was to "write a story treatment for either a sequel to *Return of the Jedi* or *Indiana Jones and the Last Crusade*." Brittany was (is) a big fan of Indiana Jones, but wasn't as into Star Wars. "Can you help me, Britt?" she asked. And so I said, "Sure, let's write a sequel to *Return of the Jedi* that is *also* a prequel to all the Indiana Jones movies." What we came up with can only be described as "Raiders of the Lost Dinosaur Planet."

It went something like this: The opening credit crawl tells us there's been a great famine in the galaxy. Everyone is starving to death and the only solution, it seems, is to actually leave the galaxy where everyone lives and go somewhere else. In a *Battlestar Galactica*–esque move, Luke, Han, Lando, and Leia pack up everybody they like into a giant unused prototype of the Death Star, which they've painted white and renamed the "Life Star." It's the size of a small planet, and it will take them across the galaxies to their new home.

Meanwhile, living inside of a volcano, a bunch of zombie Sith Lords awaken and decide they want to leave the galaxy, too. They follow the Life Star across space until it rolls up on a lush, beautiful planet in a great solar system. It's Earth! But it's

Earth during dinosaur times. Luke and company head down to the planet to think about settling it *Terra Nova* style when the new Sith attack.* Luke has a bunch of other Jedi Knights in training now, so there's a small army of folks with lightsabers. The Sith are similarly prepared. And everyone is ready to ride some dinosaurs. Meanwhile, did I mention Leia is pregnant?

While dinosaurs and lightsabers are gratuitously featured in an awesome battle scene that includes five chase sequences *and* Lando riding a pterodactyl, Leia is fighting a different battle on the Life Star against Sith stowaways. Han is fairly useless, because at this point, Leia's lightsaber skills are totally badass. But suddenly, Leia is about to go into labor. Things are looking pretty bad for the good guys, so Han decides that they'll freeze the baby in carbonite as soon as it's born. That way, no matter what happens, the baby will be safe.

Depressingly, everything does go downhill, and because I've watched *Beneath the Planet of the Apes* too many times,† the superlaser of the Life Star accidentally gets set off and zaps the atmosphere of Earth, killing the dinosaurs and everyone else. Luckily, just before this all goes down, Han and Leia's child is tucked away into a cave, safely encased in carbonite, an immortal infant. Like Captain America, only a baby from space. The coda of the movie would reveal archaeologists, circa the early 1900s, excavating a weird cavern only to discover a new-

---

* Obviously, this was way before *Terra Nova*.

† Charlton Heston destroys the Earth in the sequel to *Planet of the Apes*. Despite Earth being gone, there are amazingly three films that were direct sequels after that. All of them (set on Earth) actually even try to honor this continuity.

born baby. Suddenly, a young Sean Connery would appear (CG, obviously) and hold the baby before softly saying, "Junior." The movie ends with the baby a little older, a toddler now, playing with a big sheepdog that Sean Connery calls Indiana.

I'm not actually sure if Brittany ever ended up using that story treatment, but I do know she passed the class and is, to this day, a real live working screenwriter. I also, of course, never believed there would be a sequel to *Return of the Jedi* until now, which is why, when asked to create one, I dreamt up a joke. Like all of you, I thought Star Wars belonged to me. Even during the prequel era I was right: everybody loved Boba Fett so much that George Lucas put Boba Fett's dad in *Attack of the Clones* in 2002. See? We've been getting our way with Star Wars more than we care to admit. Now, even though we were told we'd never get to see a sequel to *Return of the Jedi*, we're somehow living in an age where that is happening, too. And these guys, unlike me, are taking it seriously. Star Wars has often been accused of being a new kind of cultural mythology, and like superheroes, I think that's relatively true. But, up until right now, it was never actually passed down to a new generation. What's been "ruining" Star Wars all these years, and what sometimes continues to "ruin" it, is its insistence on looking backward. Collectively, both the fans and George Lucas knew the classic trilogy could never be topped, so instead, we got the special edition and a glorified backstory in the form of the prequels. To actually make a sequel to *Return of the Jedi*, and by extension the "real" Star Wars movies, is much riskier and requires everyone to actually move on and leave the baggage of the old stories behind. The prequels and the special editions inherited the emotional baggage of our childlike love of the original films, and so, we didn't like them, and in fact, hated them. Hate, we're told by Yoda, leads to the Dark Side, which is probably why Star Wars has been perceived to be in need of this comeback.

Smartly, Obi-Wan Kenobi intentionally lets Luke Skywalker take over the heroic narrative of the story in *A New Hope*. And ever since then, fans around the world have longed to have that lightsaber passed to them, too. With Lucas leaving and letting younger people like J. J. Abrams and Rian Johnson actually make real Star Wars movies, it's sort of like that has happened in real life. I'm closer in age to J. J. Abrams than I am to George Lucas. J. J. Abrams and Rian Johnson are *possibly* bigger fans of Star Wars than George Lucas. This is a good thing. Things are really starting anew. The exciting thing about Star Wars is that it perpetually reminds us that everyone can have new beginnings. Everything can change; everyone can be redeemed. And now that the father of this insanely important pop event has allowed a different generation to take over, maybe the rest of us can do the same.

It's time to get over ourselves. We can stop being haters by letting go of our hate. There's still good in us. I can feel it.

ACKNOWLEDGMENTS

Something like this doesn't happen without tons of friends, colleagues, and robots-in-arms. If you feel like I forgot you, I'm sorry. I'll write your name in when I see you.

Big guns first: thanks to my agent Christopher Hermelin for believing in this book and me on nearly blind faith. To Ryan Harbage and his Fischer-Harbage Agency for making it happen. To Matthew Daddona, a brilliant editor and my favorite Rebel general. And thanks to everyone at Plume and the empire of Penguin at large. It's good to be here.

Thanks to the editors of publications where many of these pieces originally appeared or to any editor who has had the misfortune of dealing with me at all: Will Doig, Pete Smith, Neil Clarke, Cheryl Morgan, Choire Sicha, Matt Buchanan, James Yeh, Lincoln Michel, Josh Perilo, Joel Cunningham, Melissa Albert, Janet Manley, and Claire Evans.

Thanks and apologies to the early adopters who put up with me when I was a fake writer and/or a fake person: Jason

Meyer, Mike Strahan, Pat Trusela, Marsha Morris, Damon Moss, Alissa Cherry, Andy Borowitz, Vicki Lewis Thompson, Dan Kennedy, Alissa Quart, Simon Navarro, Mel Olsen, Suzanne Konig, Daniel Power, Craig Mathis, Dana, Kelly, Britt, everyone at the Gotham Writers' Workshop, Erin Harris, Seth Fishman, Sara Barron, Lyndsay Faye, Vito Grippi, Travis Kurowski, Etgar Keret, Kirsten Sorensen, Andy Christie, Ishtiaque Masud, and Asa Yappa.

Thanks to those colleagues and mentors who pushed me (knowingly or not) to be better than I am: Julia Fierro, Victor LaValle, Dani Shapiro, Michael Maren, Lev AC Rosen, James Hannaham, Jim Shepard, Karen Shepard, Hannah Tinti, John Wray, Penina Roth, Ben Greenman, Paul Park, and Lev Grossman.

A giant thank-you and some hugs and kisses and high fives and rounds of drinks go to my sci-fi family of many years, those who occupy the rocket ship of Tor.com and its related fleet; Irene Gallo, Greg Manchess, Bridget McGovern, Bridget Smith, Emily Asher-Perrin, Kelsey Ann Barrett, Sara Tolf, Patrick Nielsen-Hayden, Ellen Datlow, Carl Engle-Laird, Theresa DeLucci, Pritpaul Bains, Mordicia Knode, Diana Pho, Leah Schnelbach, Natalie Zutter, Patty Garcia, Fritz Foy, Jenny Tavis, and Chris Lough. Obviously this wouldn't exist without any of you.

To my students: So many of you have meant the world to me, but you're too many to list. My favorites know who they are. If you're reading this, you are one of my favorites.

Thanks to my friends who by just existing over the years have kept me either sane or insane depending on what we've both needed: Syreeta McFadden, Brittany Hilgers, Mike Stuto, Tracie Matthews, the Spirit of the Hi-Fi Bar, Shelly Oria,

Michael Irish, Jessica Noven, James Scott Patterson, Rob Ventre, William Irwin IV, Ted Dodson, Melissa Febos, Rebecca Keith, Jenn Abbotts, Mike Baptist, Colleen Kinder, Leslie Jamison, Emily Wunderlich, Andy Reynolds, Gabriela Vainsencher, Hugo Perez, Emily Stowe, Sam Brewer, Julie Messner, Diana Spechler, Karen Thompson Walker, Casey Walker, Leigh Stein, Robert Silva, Nathan Ihara, Hannah Labovitch, Artie Niederhoffer, Hal Hlavinka, Irene Plax, Jenny Blackman, Emily Kate O'Brien, Amanda Hess, Jenn Northington, Amanda Bullock, Justin Taylor, Adam Wilson, Janet Turley, Brett Saxon, Karen Russell, Lena Valencia, Ryan Spencer, Lindsey Skillen, Carter Edwards, Chris Togni, Anne Ray, Nelly Reifler, Teddy Wayne, Ophira Eisenberg, Jonathan Baylis, Cici James and everyone at Singularity & Co., Matt Mercier, Allegra Frazier, Stefan Merrill Block, Liese Mayer, and Justin Lemieux and the Lemieux Brood: Lucy, Caroline, and, of course, Katy.

To Wesley Allsbrook for the wonderful illustrations and limitless talent.

Thanks to Mike Lopercio, Jane M. Trayer, and the extended Trayer/Lopercio vortex, a constellation of family members who have supported me infinitely. And an extra thanks to George Lopercio for being the best and worst best friend I could ever hope for.

To my family: Mom and Kellie. You're all I've got and I don't say that enough. Of course, to the ghost of my dad, Terry Britt, who I'm sure is reading this somewhere.

And to Jillian Sanders—who thought the role of Luke Skywalker was played by Harrison Ford—this wouldn't be possible without you.

A TOTALLY INCOMPLETE GLOSSARY OF TERMS

J. J. Abrams

A cool guy whom everyone pretends they know personally, but whom nobody really knows. The new Jay Gatsby of pop-geekdom.

Isaac Asimov

A living robot who was smarter than most humans. Former president of the Humanist Society.

Back to the Future

An amazing generator of fake nostalgia. Retroactively removing this film from history would cause a paradoxical cascade effect resulting in everyone simultaneously disappearing from any Polaroid pictures that they're in. You'd still remain alive, but those old Polaroids would have weird empty spots.

Barbarella

A person who is so intentionally unrealistic that we can't even bother getting mad about it. Notice that in the face of never-ending nostalgia no one has tried to remake the movie featuring this character. You can't ruin something that already knows it's ruining itself, so no one has even tried.

Kim Catrall

Famous for *Sex and the City*, but also played Lieutenant Valeris in *Star Trek VI*. I waited on her once and told her I loved her in *Star Trek*. She was about as polite as you can imagine you might be if you received a compliment like that from someone who was pouring you a glass of wine.

Dinosaurs

A shorthand for anything that is permanently cool. Because we can't go back in time and see dinosaurs for real, their inherent awesomeness can never be taken away from us. This is what it will be like to love the Beatles in the year 2070.

Doctor Who

A pleasurable experience that has to be meticulously explained first in order to be enjoyed. It's worth it, in the end, all the explaining. But the process feels like taking inoculation vaccines before you go on vacation.

Dracula

A guy who says he's one thing, but is really something else. See: "everyone."

Harlan Ellison

Specific kind of superbeing sent down to Earth by a ruthless god, designed to test our resolve and poke fun at what we think is "creativity."

Fan Fiction

Something critics point and laugh at all the time but secretly read.

Ghostbusters

A nearly perfect film that has two flaws: the fact that it's a sausage fest and the existence of *Ghostbusters II*. That being said, if *Ghostbusters II*'s "World of the Psychic" were a real mainstream television program that Bill Murray really hosted, network television would be infinitely more watchable.

Sherlock Holmes

A proto-superhero whose superpowers were as follows: being really smart, pretending like he didn't care about sex, and possessing the ability to have a drug problem that actually assisted him in doing his job. If Sherlock Holmes habitually drank Miller High Life instead of shooting cocaine through a needle, no one would believe he was a mad "genius." They'd just think he was a drunk weirdo. The lesson? Choose to be addicted to interesting drugs.

Captain James Tiberius Kirk

A character who—just like James Bond—is only a sex symbol in the mind of the actor (Shatner) who originated the role. Until he was played by Chris Pine, and then he became a sex symbol to average people who go to movies and say things like "Did you see Chris Pine in *Horrible Bosses 2*?" Oddly, the answer to this question is always no. No one has seen that movie. Not even the people who made it.

Ursula K. Le Guin

A being of pure energy cooler than most humans, living robots, and time-traveling ghosts. The science fiction version of a saint.

George Lucas

The inverse-deadbeat dad to millions of us. He gave us Star Wars and then left us—he left us! When he returned, we became demanding, ungrateful, and bitter children. Nothing he can ever do is going to be good enough. When he left us a second time in 2012 (by selling off Star Wars), we were the happiest we've been in years.

Marvel

The Nike of geek interests. We don't know what part of our souls we're losing by consuming their products and we don't want to know.

Narnia

An overcrowded, deranged alternate world of magic that was accidentally discovered by Lev Grossman in real life. His autobiographical work, *The Magicians*, vaguely describes how awful Narnia actually was. Biggest letdown of all: Aslan was not really a lion.

Christopher Nolan

Someone who is exactly like the Batman of his films: he is a hero, but we can't wait to turn on him.

RoboCop

A guy whom I didn't really talk about in this book. I'm not sure why. Maybe it's because I love him. Oh God, please, don't get me started. It was a long time ago and I miss him terribly. Not a day goes by when I don't think of what might have been. Please. Let me be. Don't mention his name. I'll weep.

Robot

Pronounced "row-baught" if you're the vast majority of the world's population, but strangely pronounced with a frog-like "row-butt," if you're a parent or Isaac Asimov.

Steven Spielberg

Our dad's (George Lucas) cooler brother who got us high that one time on that camping trip when we were fourteen. We never talk to our cool uncle now, but we always speak in reverent tones about how awesome he was on that one camping trip.

Star Trek II: The Wrath of Khan

An old relationship we'll never get over. It was perfect and we compare all of our lovers (Star Trek movies) to this person. There's good reason for this, but we should really try to move on.

Star Wars

A crafty media hoax (created by our dad) that has convinced a lot of people that the Force, the Skywalker family, and a certain galaxy far, far away are all "fiction."

J. R. R. Tolkien

A literary hoax designed by C. S. Lewis to take the heat off of the fact that so many people were looking for the real entry points into Narnia.

Kurt Vonnegut Jr.

A time-traveling ghost of Mark Twain who has turned out to be a slightly better writer while inhabiting his "new body." Smoked cigarettes as opposed to cigars to confuse people as to his true identity.

Sigourney Weaver

One of the best actors of all time who was in two of the best science fiction movies ever made: *Ghostbusters* and *Alien*. She was also in *Avatar*.

Joss Whedon

A man famous for creating exactly two types of characters without writing any dialogue whatsoever: "The Buffy" and "The Willow." These archetypes will live on for centuries under various guises like "Tony Stark" and "Bruce Banner."

John Williams

A scientific curiosity. Apparently, there's one of these inside everyone's brain and when certain events—personal achievement, personal loss, a car chase—occur in your life (or if you witness these things in films) you'll hear theme-appropriate "music" generated magically by this phenomenon.

A NOTE ON THE ESSAYS

All essays are unique to this book, except those noted below:

Some elements of "Luke Skywalker Can't Read" previously appeared in a different form as "Most Citizens of the *Star Wars* Galaxy Are Probably Totally Illiterate," published by Tor.com in 2012.

An earlier version of "Wearing Dracula's Pants" was originally published in *Story* in 2015. Some elements of both versions derived from "Let the Snazzy One In," published by Tor.com in 2011.

Elements of "Baker Streets on Infinite Earths: Sherlock Holmes as the Eternal Sci-Fi Superhero" appeared in a different form and with different material as "Sherlock Holmes and the Science Fiction of Deduction," published by *Clarkesworld* in 2010.

Some elements of "No, Luke, *Captain Kirk* Is Your Father" appeared in "Our Dysfunctional Relationship with *The Wrath of Khan*," "How to Root for Captain Kirk," and "*Star Trek into*

Darkness Forgot to Be Literary," all published by Tor.com in 2011, 2012, and 2013, respectively. Other elements appeared originally in "Literary Star Trek Mash-Ups," published by *The Mindhut* in 2014.

Some elements of "Hipster Robots Will Save Us All" previously appeared in a different form as "Trying on the Retro Flesh," published by *OMNI Reboot* in 2013.

Elements of "Nobody Gets Mad About Hamlet Remakes: Rise of the Relevant Superheroes" appeared with the same title but in a completely different form on Tor.com in 2012. Other elements were incorporated from "Comic Book Movies and the Forgotten Art of the Ending," published by *The Awl* in 2014.